Letters to a
Young
Philosopher

# Letters to a
# Young Philosopher

Ramin Jahanbegloo

OXFORD
UNIVERSITY PRESS

# OXFORD
## UNIVERSITY PRESS

Oxford University Press is a department of the University of Oxford.
It furthers the University's objective of excellence in research, scholarship,
and education by publishing worldwide. Oxford is a registered trademark of
Oxford University Press in the UK and in certain other countries.

Published in India by
Oxford University Press
2/11 Ground Floor, Ansari Road, Daryaganj, New Delhi 110 002, India

ISBN-13: 978-0-19-948038-8
ISBN-10: 0-19-948038-9

Typeset in 10/16 Trump Mediaeval LT Std
by Excellent Laser Typesetters, Pitampura, Delhi 110 034
Printed in India by Replika Press Pvt. Ltd

*To George Steiner,*
*in gratitude*

# Contents

# Contents

# Foreword

Philosophy has had a strange history. For the ancient Athenians who invented the term and gave it a recognizable disciplinary shape, it meant love of wisdom. As they understood it, it reflected on the great goals and purposes of human existence, developed a comprehensive vision of individual and collective life, and used that vision to assess the significance or worth of different human activities. It articulated the art of living, and was the noblest and the highest form of inquiry. Christianity, which challenged Greek rationalism and made knowledge of the goals and purposes of human life a matter of divine grace and revelation, nevertheless continued to use the philosophical mode of reasoning to explain and justify its conclusions. Philosophy was now subordinated to theology, but never entirely, because it had its own logic and aspirations, and the relation between the two remained both tense and creative. A major change came with the rise of modern science which, unlike theology, had no obvious use for philosophy and which in fact it intended to replace.

In its search for a new role, philosophy became epistemology analysing, sharpening, and criticizing the central concepts and claims of science, or ethics, or turned inward and emerged as a history of philosophy. Debates between these and other views of philosophy continue, and there is no clear consensus on what it stands for. The old Greek idea of philosophy as an inquiry into the art of living still continues to hover in the background, accepted by some with enthusiasm, hesitantly embraced by some others, and dismissed by several contemporaries as an act of ancient piety lacking intellectual weight.

Ramin Jahanbegloo is an advocate of the Greek view of philosophy. Arguing that life is unimaginable without thinking, that all serious thinking is probing, truthful, systematic, and interrelated, that this is what philosophy endeavours to do, and that it therefore represents directly or indirectly the telos of all thinking about human life. Jahanbegloo exemplifies this by reflecting on great themes of human existence such as wisdom, love, death, friendship, empathy, peace, and reconciliation, analyses them with care, discusses what kind of life is worth living, and offers a fascinating vision of a reflective and truthful life.

Since human life is marked by pressure for conformity, intellectual superficiality, moral shallowness, and venality, philosophy is for him basically a voice of protest, of resistance. As an inquiry committed to finding the meaning of life by critical and truthful thinking, it must challenge established orthodoxies, conventional mediocrities. And the cluster of clichés to which so much of our public discourse is reduced. These act as conceptual gate keepers channelling our thoughts and feelings in certain directions and denuding them of their freshness and vitality. For Jahanbegloo, a philosopher is necessarily a gadfly, whose job is to sting his contemporaries and keep them in a state of full alertness.

This is a fine book, full of wisdom, insights and subtle distinctions. Like a good philosophical work, it both stings and from time to time invites disagreement. Some professional philosophers might worry about the intellectual and moral burden it places on them, and ask for a fuller account and defence of the author's view of philosophy as the 'supreme domain' bringing together diverse manners of looking at reality and combining various fields of knowledge. Some other critics might take issue with his views on love, death, friendship, and empathy, all fascinating but a little hurried in places. Yet others might find the work a little too one-sided and wish to know more about the reactions of the addressee to the sometimes rather high-minded pronouncements of his senior interlocutor. The addressee evolves from 'My dear young colleague' to 'My young friend', 'My dear philosophical companion', and so on, each reflecting an increasing degree of intellectual intimacy that remains unexplained in the absence of his responses.

Jahanbegloo is aware of this, and is able to answer these and related criticisms. One hopes that he will now write a companion volume of similar depth and ambition constructed in a dialogical and argumentative form. This book has whetted the reader's appetite and prepared the necessary ground for it.

BHIKHU PAREKH
House of Lords
London, April 2017

# Preface

## Philosophy in Dark Times

I have always loved reading philosophers. It didn't matter to me if they were ancient or modern, religious or non-religious, oriental or western. Undoubtedly, philosophers, more than economists, lawyers, or politicians, have held my gaze as a teenager or later as an adult. Philosophy, itself, came to matter to me up to a point that I continued to learn it at different stages of my life, but also to teach it to others. Philosophy, as the love of wisdom, had become for me a way of life. When we say philosophy is a way of life, we mean a certain dwelling in the world and in one's historical time. Unsurprisingly, philosophers themselves had a good sense of their zeitgeist in which their

life and destiny came together. Hegel understood
this perfectly when he said 'Philosophy is its
time apprehended in thoughts'. This is no small
observation, and yet I believe it is still a big goal
well worth pursuing. As a way of life, but also as
a mode of thinking, philosophy and philosophers
have taken the responsibility of asking perennial
questions for over twenty-six centuries: What
is the meaning of life? What is justice? What is
happiness? How can human beings live together?
Does God exist? What can I know? What ought I
to do? What may I hope? And so on. No wonder
why history of philosophy is the story of men
and women who agonized in asking questions
like these. For nearly three thousand years, philosophers, as well-established social figures, had a
great impact on the evolution of ideas in human
history. As such, despite what people say and
think today, philosophical ideas made the world
and changed the course of the world. For a long
time, to philosophize was to think differently and
dangerously. And to be a philosopher was to attest
to the close relation between the quests for mean-

ing and for truth. Arendt compares thinking to Penelope's ruse of unweaving the shroud in order to wait for the return of Odysseus. 'The business of thinking,' says Arendt, 'is like Penelope's web: it undoes every morning what it has finished the night before'. Arendt's concern with the value of thinking beyond knowing, by incessantly asking questions about our lives is also intrinsic to our social responsibility as political beings. Thus, the absence of a relentless questioning, which has been the main task of philosophy, is at the same time the failure of giving meaning to our world. Far from being just a set of clever questions, the act of philosophizing is to ask the everlasting Socratic question: in which way should one live? Doing philosophy today means obviously more than participating in what we call 'philosophical debates'. It means leading a philosophical life. This does not seem to be the case here and now.

Ask the question—or perhaps merely overhear it, for it is already asked frequently—what is the place of philosophy in today's world, and you will inevitably hear a variety of contradictory responses. Nevertheless, philosophy is probably named most often as a form of knowledge, which is found in the writings of past philosophers, and is of no value in a world taken over by science and technology. This is, however, only a short glimpse of how citizens of today's world consider philosophical thinking. The criticism aimed at philosophy, in a word, does not concern its existence, but it is a matter of its utility in our world. And yet, philosophy unlike technology has never been concerned by the spirit of utility. In other words, if philosophy has any value at all in the twenty-first century, it is only because it is not about anything except thinking philosophically. Philosophy does not exist for anything. It is an end in itself. As such, even if all the problems of today's world were solved and we had no more poverty, illiteracy, violence, and wars, we would still seek philosophical knowledge. This is encapsulated in Socrates's vision of life as an endless self-examination. Socratic self-examination stresses the necessity of philosophical questioning not only in schools, colleges, and universities, but mainly in the Agora, the marketplace, where people can talk to each other and discuss norms and values. One important idea that Socrates questioned was that of justice. Socratic inquiry is also that of history of philosophy, a wake-up call for the passive minds of citizens who would prefer the dogmatic assurance of conformity and complacency to a tightrope on which philosophical interrogation has walked for over twenty-six centuries.

Thus, the mind which has become accustomed to instrumental and calculative thinking, cannot think of philosophical interrogation as not being a referential discourse like all sciences. It follows from this account that philosophical questioning has more in common with the pure exercise of thinking itself, than just as a form of knowing which brings solutions to the problems. As a matter of fact, while not considering itself as superior to art or science, philosophy does imply a distinction between knowing and thinking. In this, as in many things, philosophy can be a troublesome activity for the self and for society. As Hannah Arendt underlines majestically, 'Thinking is always out of order, interrupts all ordinary activities and is interrupted by them'. The thinking experience, unlike knowing, manifests itself from our questioning of the world. Obviously, if there is no urge or courage of thinking, there can be no art of questioning, that is, philosophy. But that we are in possession of a knowledge does not necessarily mean that we are also in quest for meaning, which is 'meaningless' to whatever is not philosophy. As Arendt says, 'the questions raised by thinking and which it is in reason's very nature to raise—questions of meaning—are all unanswerable by common sense and the refinement of it we call science'. In this, as in many things, philosophy stood and continues to stand as an example of the true life of thinking that knows neither joy nor glory.

Truth is that philosophy is an act of resistance against lies and hypocrisy. From the point of view of the French philosopher Gilles Deleuze, 'Philosophy isn't a power: religions, States, capitalism, science, the law, public opinion, and ... with the powers that be, but it does fight a war without battles—a guerrilla campaign—against them'. It is perhaps for the same reason that Kant claimed the phrase *sapere aude* (dare to think) as the battle cry of philosophical thought against prejudice, ignorance, and dogmatism. Let us be clear, there is another side to having the courage to use one's own reason in the public space; it is an effort to think thoughtlessness. It is this absence of thinking which has become so ordinary an act in our everyday life that is at the root of disinterest of younger generations in philosophy. Therefore, the question that comes to mind is: could the absence of thinking as such, the absence of questioning reality, in direct relation to a worrying trend of complacency and conformism among citizens of the world? To put it differently: is the decline of philosophy in our world reinforcing the rise of evil?

Seen from this perspective the effort of philosophizing is a moral task of taming violence in our world. The lesson here is to avoid the arrogance of meaninglessness, while distancing oneself from utopianism, especially of the variety that leads to thinking that a worldly paradise is possible.

Along with thinking, excellence is the essential value to a philosopher, whether for creative purposes or simply for living. But excellence can be considered possible only in the context of an education through which excellence is fostered. The Athenians believed that excellence breeds excellence. So striving for excellence for its own sake, for truth, beauty, and goodness in the whole educational process, was considered as the only way to produce it. This is no more where we stand. Education in today's world does not provide us anymore with the conditions to learn excellence. It is no more about character building, but about diploma seeking. For the ancients, there was no other training than philosophy that was more likely to lead to excellence. Maybe that is why they used the word *humanitas* to describe the refining or humanizing effects of a broad education in the liberal arts.

When asked why they teach, many academics would suggest that teaching is a preparation for life. However, one can say that the academia, as a domain for education of human beings, is not only a place for the preparation of life, but life itself. If that is the case, we need, therefore, to review and rethink the priority of academic education in today's world. The truth is that it seems absolutely absurd for a philosopher to teach philosophy just to end up getting a salary at the end of the month. Also, it is equally meaningless for students of philosophy to go to philosophy classes in order to have a degree and enter the job market. Philosophy is not a job, it is a vocation. You do not study it in the same way that you study corporate law. Maybe this is the reason why greatness of soul is not fostered by corporate leaders and lawyers in our world of unreason and violence. Therefore, as Bertrand Russell puts it clearly,

Philosophy is to be studied, not for the sake of any definite answers to its questions, since no definite answers can, as a rule, be known to be true, but rather for the sake of the questions themselves; because these questions enlarge our conception of what is possible, enrich our intellectual imagination and diminish the dogmatic assurance which closes the mind against speculation; but above all because, through the greatness of the universe which philosophy contemplates, the mind also is rendered great, and becomes capable of that union with the universe which constitutes its highest good.

There was a time, not long ago, when teaching philosophy meant having high ideals for humanity that prized freedom, human dignity, and moral worth. It was also a time when being a philosopher meant living in truth and for truth, and placing excellence as a virtue before pleasures and gains in life. But it seems as if today law schools and business schools are flourishing all over the world, where boorish and uneducated corporate bureaucrats can decide if a department of philosophy should continue existing or being replaced by an institute for behavioural sciences. The bitter truth is that corporate power which is nowadays dominating and controlling universities and institutes around the world thinks in terms of a competitive society, one that divides people into winners and losers. This attitude of mind can barely represent a moral ideal with which nation building begins and with which humanity survives. Let me place it out bluntly: philosophy cannot survive without a noble attitude to life which has always been exemplified by an effort to overcome mediocrity and immaturity. Philosophy is not an institution of flattery and adulation, but a life of questioning and critical thinking. As such, there can be no philosophy without a real life of the mind.

'So few that live have life,' wrote Emily Dickinson. Assuredly, for a poet a non-meaningful life is indeed an original sin. Poets, like philosophers, they do not invite us to be perfect. They invite us to have a meaningful life, which is about living our lives as nobly and as ideally as possible. 'The task is to think life', as Hegel wrote and his French commentator Jean Hyppolite was particularly fond of repeating after him. Here is where this book starts. Inspired by Rainer Maria Rilke's *Letters to a Young Poet*, written from 1903 to 1908 as a series of deep and lucid responses to Franz Kappus, a young, would-be poet, who was about to enter the German military, these letters to a young philosopher follow the same tone of friendship and the same quest of beauty and truth. The simplicity of Rilke's writing is the legacy of his poetic thinking, a legacy which he himself inherited from the tradition of thought which preceded him. This is what he writes to the young poet:

Have patience with everything that remains unsolved in your heart. Try to love the questions themselves, like locked rooms and like books written in a foreign language. Do not now look for the answers. They cannot now be given to you because you could not live them. It is a question of experiencing everything. At present you need to live the question. Perhaps you will gradually, without even noticing it, find yourself experiencing the answer, some distant day.

In a very real sense, there is no beginning and ending in poetry and philosophy, since everything is a great becoming. Heidegger writes, *'Alles is weg'* ('Everything is way'). Hence, if philosophy has to be the chosen path, it needs to be called in us as an act of thinking. But the call of philosophy is heard only as long as there are those who can hear it.

RAMIN JAHANBEGLOO
New Delhi, 6 April 2017

# One

## On the Definition of Philosophy

Toronto, 12 January 2008

My dear young colleague,

Your letter arrived while I was travelling to Medellin. I, therefore, apologize for my late response to your mail. However, I am extremely delighted and immensely joyful to receive a letter from a young philosopher (some people have problems with this title because for them you cannot be young and a philosopher at the same time) and to share your views on the love of wisdom and the world that surrounds it.

Let me start by saying that I cherish your confidence for my writings and I am grateful for the sympathy and interest that you express for my life and works. I do not pretend to have an inexhaustibly fertile mind, but one can find an element of versatility in my writings, since my interest for various cultures and traditions of thought have been immense. However, life is not long enough for the achievement of all tasks of thought and action and for what we can learn from life itself.

I am wholly convinced that philosophy is the supreme domain which brings together various fields of knowledge and diverse manners of looking at reality. It is not hard to see that philosophical interrogation has accompanied humanity from its first civilizational steps in the hanging gardens of Babylon and around the columns of Acropolis. No one can say exactly when and where the first human being started to philosophize, but more than anything else the manner in which this interrogation was realized through a deep existential astonishment before the world reminds us of what the pre-Socratic philosophers singled out as *apeiron*, or a principle of all beginnings.

Anaximander describes 'apeiron' as a kind of matrix for all generated things and the Pythagoreans considered it as the 'unlimited'. This principle with no limits was described by the Greeks to have no beginning or an end and to be indestructible and immortal. If apeiron is of the essence of a mystery for the pre-Socratic philosophers, and above all of the *Mysterium Magnum*, that it emerges as something divine, that it possesses an element of indefiniteness, then, as Aristotle says, it cannot exist as an actual being, but only as a potentiality and a possibility.

According to Aristotle, 'the unlimited is the open possibility of taking more, however much you have already taken; that of which there is nothing more to take is not unlimited, but whole or completed'. Unlimitedness is, after all, a principal component of one's concept of infinity. And infinity is the boundless origin of all that is. As the Upanishads say, if we take away infinite from infinity, infinity is not reduced in any way, because one cannot take away anything from infinity. Therefore, what lies at the end of the road is what is already there at its beginning. As Wittgenstein formulates it beautifully, 'what is infinite about endlessness is only the endlessness itself'. To have no end is to be continuous. We say something is continuous when it is unbroken and uninterrupted.

Theologians hold to the notion of continuity as a chain of being, meaning if God exists, there is a continuity of being between God and Man. That in turn implies an understanding of the meaning of the natural order that God has decreed for man. In other words, Man is at his place in the Great Chain of Being and 'Whatever is, is right' as says Alexander Pope in his *Essay on Man*. But we know that Voltaire picked this up and made a mockery out of it in his *Candide*. According to him, Master Pangloss could prove admirably that, 'All is for the best in the best of all possible worlds'. The acid relevance of Voltaire is not only that his work is highly inflammatory and critical, a spirit which is fully needed by a young philosopher like you, but also that every philosophical movement involves the civic task of changing the inherited face of a society and its institutions.

Being a philosopher means not conforming to the general attitude which often looks for the meaning of life in what is set before it. As Oscar Wilde strongly asserts, 'there are moments when one has to choose between living one's own life, fully, entirely, completely—or dragging out some false, shallow, degrading existence that the world in its hypocrisy demands'. This is your philosophical moment now. If you have sorrows, if you have existential pains, do not blame philosophy. First, blame the world in which you live. Second, blame the sheep mentality that kills and destroys all form of questioning. Masses do not need questions because they have no doubts about anything. And they have no doubts because they judge things as good or bad without thinking about them. It would be wrong and un-philosophical to pretend that philosophy has all the answers.

But philosophy takes the time to think about questions which come as absolute certainties to the masses. So a reflection is philosophical and meditative if it has sprung from the act of questioning. As a philosopher, you must take the destiny of thinking upon yourself and bear its burden of questioning, without ever asking if this is a way to celebrity. Now, I beg you to understand that philosophers do not philosophize in order to become famous. There are so many ways to celebrity in our world which are of no interest to a philosopher. Therefore, avoid mediocrity and celebrity as you avoid pest, cholera, and Ebola. You remember what the Greeks said about infinity. It is the same for philosophy.

Philosophy is the infinite way of thinking. If we take away philosophers from philosophy, philosophy is not reduced in any way, because one cannot take away the possibility of thinking from philosophy. Philosophy must be a world in itself and for itself, and find everything in itself. This is how your life as a young philosopher finds its own way thence and this is how you will keep growing quietly but surely. There is much more that I can say to you, but after all you will need to reflect alone on your philosophical life. Do not forget, philosophy is a mirror and will reflect back to the philosopher what she thinks into it.

Truly yours
R

# Two

## On the Decline of Education

Delhi, 25 March 2008

My young friend,

Some twelve days ago I left Toronto, tired of its long and depressing winters and disenchanted by its falsely snobbish and non-philosophical environment. I feel more human since my arrival in Delhi and enjoy mixing with a spiritual and empathic environment whose air and colours bring me back my moral health and my taste of writing. I am using this first moment of intellectual joy and rejuvenation to greet you and to demand forgiveness for not having responded to your letter earlier. It was your letter of 5 February, and you surely remember the main points you made in it. When I read it, as now, in the great serenity of these surroundings, I am touched by your beautiful concern about philosophy, in these times of philosophical decline.

You must know that every letter of yours gives me pleasure and hope as the view of a life boat to a castaway in an ocean of mediocrity. Your kind letter does not fail through your questions to make it clear to me that teaching philosophy in a world which has abandoned the art of thinking is not an easy task. You ask me if I have always enjoyed teaching philosophy. I beg you to understand that philosophy has been my greatest love in life. I confess that I have never had a more romantic relation with anyone as I had it with the world of philosophy. Nothing has been a greater source of consolation and hope as a page of Pascal, Hegel, Schopenhauer, or Nietzsche. Therefore, I would say, with nothing can one approach a work of philosophy lesser than with a lack of love and passion. This is a lesson that very few of my colleagues and students understand, since for a great number of them grades, exams, diplomas, and jobs precede the passion of thinking and the art of learning. As Schopenhauer underlines, 'In philosophy at the universities truth occupies only a secondary place and, if called upon, she must get up and make room for another attribute'. I can assure you that if a Jean-Paul Sartre or an Albert Camus were applying for a job position at the philosophy or political science departments in the US or Canada, they would probably be rejected by a committee of bureaucratic philistines. I tell you, nothing is more exhausting than the snobbish philistinism of bureaucrats who take themselves seriously. It's incredible that in our time you can walk into a philosophy or a political science department and the only things you don't hear your colleagues and students talk about are philosophy and politics. I beg you not to spend too much time at North American universities, otherwise instead of having a metaphysical existence you will become an animal of paperwork and regulations. This is what Winston Churchill had in mind when he mentioned, 'If you have ten thousand regulations you destroy all respect for the law'. And this further: do not think that philosophy is only taught at universities. We are no more in the Middle Ages and universities are no more spaces for great spirits. Alas, universities function in today's world as insurance companies and professors are just a group of insurance officers gathered around a fundraiser who worries more about the number of endowments and grants rather than the intellectual future of the students. And then what? What does thinking have to do with this half-battered existence which they call teaching or studying? Everything is incubation and then bringing forth. Thinking is difficult, yes. But it is not more difficult than living. We need to await with deep humility and patience the germination of thoughts. But it seems that this humility is replaced by a hurried arrogance of success. Listen to what Nietzsche has to say on this:

Success has always been the greatest liar—and the 'work' itself is a success; the great statesman, the conqueror, the discoverer is disguised by his creations, often beyond recognition; the 'work,' whether of the artist or the philosopher, invents the man who has created it, who is supposed to have created it; 'great men,' as they are venerated, are subsequent pieces of wretched minor fiction.

Do not be confused by the multiplicity of individuals who talk about being successful. These people are the white pages of history. Do not be bewildered by those who live on the surfaces. Look in the depths and that is where you will find true thinkers. Let philosophy live in you like a soul mate. Let your philosophical motto be 'Resistance'. Resistance against conformism. Resistance against immaturity. You should know that no philosopher has ever served freethinking without resisting laziness of thought and mediocrity. We live essentially in an age of calculative and instrumental thinking, and yet technological progress and development goes ahead with an ever increasing tempo of idiotization. There is great deal of technology all over our world and people talk about it loudly. There is nothing strange about talking loudly of technology, business, and politics. It is through their noise making that they exist and dominate our planet. But as Jawaharlal Nehru says in one of his speeches, 'Culture is not loud; it is quiet, it is restrained, it is tolerant'. I do not deny at all, having certain sympathy for all these Indians who understand things in the larger context of life. I have infinite faith in some creative minds who live among us and have the capacity to go beyond the herd mentality which destroys all the best qualities of human beings as great creators of art, philosophy, and science. But it is painful to feel all the time that while humanity holds its great heritage of ideals, unrefined and uncultured characters come in the way and turn back the clock to barbarism. This is why I think we live no more in the period of crisis, but in the time of philosophical emergency. Whether we are lucid and wise enough to face it adequately or not is another matter. Yet, I find a strange lack of awareness of this fact. Maybe it's time to repeat the Kantian dictum of *Sapere Aude* (Have the courage to use your own understanding). I invite you to meditate on this thought until our next correspondence.

Yours ever

R

# Three

## On Living with the Technological Civilization

Beijing, 30 April 2008

My dear philosophical companion,

As you can see I am sending you this letter from China. It's so unfortunate to see such a rich and beautiful civilization converted into a vast capitalist factory in the name of progress and power. The open-door economy has resulted in massive urban change accompanied with congested and polluted cities. As a matter of fact, progress and power are two words that have reduced our world into a heartless production process with no substance. Progress, as we are experiencing it today, begins wherever someone looks at a factory or a multinational corporation and thinks: they are only doing their job. But as Theodor Adorno says, 'There is no right life in the wrong one'. So, I ask you, where is the spirit of rage and revolt against this barbarity? Well, the truth, my young friend, is that one must have a passion of questioning in oneself, to reject and refuse vehemently the damaged and decayed momentum with which we are living today. Going back to the Chinese civilization and its contributions to human history, I think that we need to consider the fact that the Chinese rose above their limitations. Like all other great civilizations of the past, they managed to erect intellectual, artistic, scientific, and political structures that transcended the simplicity of their daily lives and provided templates for the future of humanity. The crucial question the Chinese asked themselves—one that future generations of Chinese have also pondered is: what made the Chinese great? Well, my friend, the answer is provided by this poem of 1927 by Wen Yiduo: 'Please tell me, who are the Chinese? Show me how to cherish memory. Please tell me of this people's greatness. Softly tell me, don't shout it out.' Here we see the tension between memory and progress. How should we cherish the memory of civilizations past? I merely hear the voice of the past civilization in the noisy military parades of the Tiananmen Square. It seems to me that reading Confucius and Lao Tzu in our tough, cynical, and merciless global environment is like hearing echoes of lost hopes and dreams. As such, faith or even a simple interest in progress is ironical in a century ravaged by boredom, violence, and meaninglessness. Living with the technological civilization is an insult to civilization itself and a mockery of happiness. Let me take you with me to my territory of consciousness and ask you to meditate shortly with me on what happiness could mean for us in the twenty-first century. Frankly, since the time I started studying philosophy seriously, I agreed with Epicurus that the purpose of philosophy was to attain the happy life, characterized by *ataraxia*, peace and freedom from fear, and *aponia*, the absence of pain. Yet, someone like St. Thomas Aquinas would say in answer to Epicurus, that humankind's ultimate happiness does not consist in philosophizing or in acts of pleasure; it consists in the contemplation of God. I always believed that I contemplate happiness without contemplating God, but I never thought of happiness without spirituality. Human beings are spiritual animals and that is why they fear death and hope beyond death. All animals live in the present, but humans are the only creatures that live in and with the future. As Pascal says majestically,

We almost never think of the present, and if we do think of it, it is only to see what light it throws on our plans for the future. The present is never our end. The past and the present are our means, the future alone our end. Thus we never actually live, but hope to live, and since we are always planning how to be happy, it is inevitable that we should never be so.

If we agree with Pascal, humans are unhappy because they are unsatisfied with what they are and what they have. In other words, we find relief from the pain of life in the pursuit of happiness, not in happiness itself. 'We like the chase better than the quarry,' says Pascal. Happiness is not in the mode of being, but in the act of becoming. The very essence of human being is in the act of becoming. Therefore, we are not born free, we become free. As Albert Camus says brilliantly, 'The only way to deal with an unfree world is to become so absolutely free that your very existence is an act of rebellion'. I agree with Camus that we will never be happy if we try to define happiness. What gives meaning to our lives is our rebellion against the meanings of life. Nowadays, we live with the illusion that happiness is well-being and consumption. The more we buy, the more we possess, the more we consume, and the more we are happy. But happiness is actually nothing than a moment of rebellion. Rebellion, unlike well-being, is not quantifiable and does not become an object of statistics. The aim of life is thinking and the aim of thinking is the refusal to submit.

At this point I see you smiling while reading my letter. You would say to yourself: *This old man is insane, he has become a revolutionary.* But let me tell you frankly, if at times I seem to choose the path of pessimism, this is because I simply need to think against the tide, and not because I put my happiness before my love for truth. I do not believe in revolutions. Revolutions do not cancel tyrants and gods; they create new ones. But I think it is a great deal to be a rebel while despising violence, to be suspicious of heroes, while cherishing the idea of a heroic civilization. We have much to overcome—and first of all the hypocritical image we have formed of mankind, as a race of thoughtless animals that is only concerned with the pursuit of wealth and pleasure. That is why we need to accept philosophy as a nonviolent sword, making sure that the spirit of rebellion and refusal is not exiled in despair. The contemporary form of true rebellion lies in a civilization founded on the spirituality of nonviolence. Let me, for once, finish on this note of optimism.

I hope my letters from abroad have been satisfactory for you. They are not, however, satisfactory to me, I confess, because they breathe a strong spirit of regret for not having met you.

Yours affectionately
R

# Four

## On the Art of Loving

Toronto, 12 May 2008

My dearest R,

I just returned to Toronto, the most unexciting city in North America. Some Torontonians revel with money making in their town's vaunted boredom. I suppose their lives swing like a pendulum backward and forward between boredom and meaninglessness. I already miss the colours and odours of Asia. It's strange, we never think of our odourless and colourless everyday lives in Canada. The bleached-out mentality has created a false sense of multiculturalism among us. We live in a society of hyphenated identities and each community has created its own ethnic enclave where its culture is isolated from all others. It seems to me that the slogan 'I am Canadian!' really should now be replaced with the true Montesquieuvian interrogation: '*Comment peut-on etre Canadien?*' (How can one be Canadian?). Your letter, however, helped to relieve my boredom. Thanks again for keeping me posted about your activities.

I was glad to see your beautiful handwriting once again. Your letter arrived some time after date, but I received the book you sent me sound and safe. I hope you do not find me ungrateful in not immediately acknowledging it. I was extremely happy to see both the letter and the book. But your letter gave me great joy. I find it strange that since the invention of the Internet and the new communication systems people have stopped sending letters to each other. Actually the most tragic is that they are losing the habit of receiving and reading letters. But never mind that, we have more important things to talk about. Your letter showed some signs of romance, but I would like to know more about your true feelings concerning the girl you have met recently in your philosophy class. Are you truly in love with her or you think that she is agreeable and you feel comfortable in her presence? If you are looking for a word of advice from an older man like me, who had many unhappy experiences with love and women, let me tell you to be careful not to idealize too much the love of your choice. This reminds me of an essay by Freud entitled, 'Group Psychology and the Analysis of the Ego', where he compares being in love with being under the effects of hypnosis. Freud says, 'From being in love to hypnosis is evidently only a short step. The respects in which the two agree are obvious. There is the same humble subjection, the same compliance, the same absence of criticism, towards the hypnotist just as towards the loved object.' Of course, in this essay Freud is talking about the reasons why love and hypnosis are both very crucial to the formation of groups and how they both replace the individual's ego ideal. But I am more concerned with what

Freud calls 'idealization' which according to him 'falsifies our judgement'. To love is a great human adventure, but to idealize is a great illusion. If we investigate the lives of individuals in today's world, we realize that we all live with the tragic illusion of obeying the moment. This is a Panglossian optimism that is no more comic. We believe in the best of all possible worlds, not because we are optimistic, but because we cannot think of other choices. I believe we have the same situation in a marriage or a love affair where partners continue to remain together because they think love and marriage are sacred institutions. But I don't think a person can be a fully spiritual being through erotic love or even through marriage. Love is the spiritual experience of living every minute without a spirit of egoism and selfishness. However, marriage turns people into selfish and destructive creatures. Do you remember this quote from Act 3, Scene 3 of Shakespeare's *Othello*? 'Oh, curse of marriage. That we can call these delicate creatures ours. And not their appetites! I had rather be a toad. And live upon the vapour of a dungeon.'

Othello's determination to punish Desdemona for cheating on him stems from his sense of conservative morality which still exists in many societies around the world. I abhor honour killings, which are done in the name of pride, traditions, or identity, but I continue to believe that marriage is not an institution that procures happiness. How about love? Does love secure us happiness? Well, it all depends on how we define love and how we define happiness. For Mahatma Gandhi, 'Happiness is when what you think, what you say, and what you do are in harmony'. So, happiness is being in harmony with oneself and the world. But let us go back to love. Love is multiple because there are many ways of loving. Love is lived in a plural way. There is a love which is a passion of possessing something or someone. Surprisingly, erotic love is a possessive passion. We can summarize it as 'I love you, therefore you are mine'. Philosophy is, also literally, a form of love. It's love of wisdom. But is love of wisdom, in any way, comparable with the love of sports or love of wealth? With philosophy, love is a quest. It's a never-ending process. With sports and wealth, it's a goal. With philosophy, it's not what you love that matters, it's the path that you cross that makes the difference. Don't forget, it's much easier to gain than to seek. An open heart and an open mind are the only believable signs of a true love. But do we need to attain wisdom to understand love or love should prevail crudely and instinctively without any quest of wisdom? Well, let me put it this way: I have never met a wise person who is not in love with life. This may be because wisdom is the art of living, even though billions of people around the world continue living without being wise or seeking wisdom. So, we go back to the very first question: why should we love? And the answer would be: in order to live. However, the first question is followed by a second one: how should we live? This is a question that love unlike wisdom, is incapable to answer. There is a Zen saying, 'Slow down and the thing you are chasing will come around and catch you'. Most of the people miss their share of life, not because they never look for it, but because they never slow down to recognize it. So dwell on the beauty of love, but do not forget to have power over your desires. As Marcus Aurelius says, 'The happiness of your life depends upon the quality of your thoughts'. You will excuse my frankness, for I am your friend, and walking with a friend in honesty is better than walking alone in hypocrisy. But I am anxious to read you on this subject. I hope to hear from you soon.

Amicably
R

# Five

## On Freedom and Courage

Bangkok, 2 June 2008

My dear philosopher,

I am sending you this letter one day before leaving for India. Thank you for your letter which brought me the greatest joy. I took it with me to Thailand, a beautiful country with beautiful people. I am happier than I have ever been, and I owe that joy to you. I cannot describe the infinite immensity of my delight to see you sharing with me your heart and mind. I apologize if my last letter caused you sorrow. However, though I regret it, I see that you are taking a fresh look at the subjects we discussed. I understand perfectly your point on the subject of freedom. If I understood you well, your definition of freedom is to expose yourself to your deepest desires. We all want to be free and we all desire to expose, but even when we expose our desires, we still desire to be free. It is because freedom is something more than desire or will. As Martin Heidegger says, 'Freedom is only to be found where there is burden to be shouldered'. Freedom is not born out of an easy road of luxury or conformity. It is born out of the experience of deep human tragedies and extraordinary political accomplishments. It is, therefore, an opening of opportunity to greater triumphs and acceptance of challenges that await us in future. Moreover, freedom is when we know that the past is over and an unending beckons to us now. This is how Nehru describes such a moment of freedom:

That future is not one of ease or resting but of incessant striving so that we might fulfill the pledges we have so often taken and the one we shall take today.... The ambition of the greatest man of our generation has been to wipe every tear from every eye. That may be beyond us but so long as there are tears and suffering, so long our work will not be over.

I am not one of those who long for the suffering of people around the world in order to obtain their freedom, while I am swinging on my rocking chair and smoking my pipe. There are already too many dead in the short history of the twenty-first century that we must try to spare all human lives we can while fighting for the cause of freedom. However, understand me well, there can be no compromise with any form of tyranny as there can be no resignation towards injustice. I hope with all my strength that the mute humanity that we have become can still recognize the shadow of tyranny behind so-called 'democratic' manners. I believe in these words of John Dryden: 'Of all the tyrannies on human kind the worst is that which persecutes the mind'. But if tyranny can corrupt human thought, a thoughtless person can also corrupt political power. The truth is that politics in today's world is reduced to what George Orwell called 'tearing human minds to pieces and putting them together again in new shapes of your own'. The idea, still voiced among many, that politics, because it is electoral, can enjoy the title of 'democratic' is an idea of those who either think no more about politics or feel inferior and incapable of transforming the order of things. But in the end, let's not forget that human beings are also capable of stretching out their hands and grasping courage. It's the great merit of a theorist like Hannah Arendt to have understood this. She says,

It requires courage even to leave the protective security of our four walls and enter the public realm, not because of particular dangers which may lie in wait for us, but because we have arrived in a realm where the concern for life has lost its validity. Courage liberates men from their worry about life for the freedom of the world. Courage is indispensable because in politics not life but the world is at stake.

If politics belongs to anyone in this world, it certainly does not belong to those who define it uniquely as power making. If, as Arendt says, we need to have courage to leave the protective security of our private lives and enter the public realm, it is not because we want to increase the sum of our interests and advantages, but because we need to insert our work in the world that we build in common with other human beings. Today, just as yesterday, politics should be the living image of our passions and sufferings. After all, the human world is a function of relations of passions and compassions.

My dear colleague, let me just say from the bottom of my heart, in the battles of our time, philosophers need to be on the side of those who have the aim to increase the sum of freedom and thought. This cannot, under any circumstance, be reduced to a mystified reality in the name of a half-truth. This is precisely the question that Camus argues when he says, 'Liberty is the way, and the only way, of perfectibility. Without liberty heavy industry can be perfected, but not justice or truth.' Now, my friend, which one is more important to you: comfort or liberty? Certainly, I understand that a philosopher, like everyone else, should go on living and enjoying the necessity of time, without going to prison or dying if possible. However, in my opinion, there aren't many ways of thinking philosophically in the world today. To think today is to think dangerously. Otherwise, philosophy is nothing but an illusory and misleading luxury of mind. Consequently, there is nothing surprising in the fact that philosophy is not popular, though thinking is possible to all of us. As a result, philosophers who reject today's thoughtless society and its spectatorship are caught in a painful dilemma: they must be conformists or marginalized and jobless. But after all there is a bigger dilemma, which is that of our contemporary world: living with illusion or dying of truth. In other words, our unbroken burden as to our freedom cannot be suspended. There is no freedom without truth. So my conclusion is simple: try to accept the fact that a philosopher is always a public enemy, even in the best of all worlds, or may I add, especially in the best of all worlds.

Adieu
R

# Six

## On the Political Evil

Toronto, 23 June 2008

Dear Mr Rainer,

I was happy to find your letter on the day of my return from India. It is a rare joy nowadays, under the domination of the empire of technology, to receive letters composed by human hands. I can even smell the ink that covers your letters and the back of the envelopes. I read your thoughts and see them develop in front of my eyes, in all their anguished art of questioning and their sweet complexity.

If I may summarize your letter, I would say that its centrepiece is the problem of the political evil. Your suggestion that we need to consider Socrates's trial and death as the first act of the genealogy of political evil in human history is an interesting point. Philosophers cannot really think about philosophy and politics or even culture without remembering that all this began in the ancient world under the sign of an injustice. An injustice was committed in Athens in 399 BC. The Athenians asked for the death of a great philosopher who according to them was corrupting the spirit of the youth. We cannot forget this injustice. This means that when we try to think about philosophy and its history, but also about politics, we know that the question of the trial and death of Socrates is always an issue.

As a matter of fact, speaking of the political evil is putting the accent on that which is criminal and unjust in politics. That is what has made the memory of the death of Socrates so traumatic for generations of philosophers. The imprisonment and assassination of philosophers is a sad fact of human history. But the trial and death of a philosopher such as Socrates, because he was a philosopher, and in the name the Athenian city state, is a radical event in the history of philosophical thought and political action.

This brings us back to what we have already discussed in our exchange of letters and that is the role of thinking in general and philosophy in particular. Thinking, as I have repeated in many of my writings, is a necessary condition for moral and political progress. The reason why our world is suffering from a moral decline is because human civilization has stopped thinking on his conditions of survival. I am sure you are familiar with this quote of my favourite Spanish philosopher, Jose Ortega Y. Gasset: 'We do not live to think, but, on the contrary, we think in order that we may succeed in surviving.' The survival that Ortega Y. Gasset is talking about is not that of the fittest, which is the foundation of all our political and economic systems, but that of human beings as members of a thinking species. Our world is beautiful because of its rich biodiversity, but also because human civilizations have always practised a sense of the beautiful. A true ability to think about beauty has enabled us to build our multiple civilizations and to learn from them. Now it's time to think anew in order to be able to resurrect our human civilization. That is why thinking, as a philosophical-meditative task, is an act of redemption. For the simple reason that there is no philosophical thinking into which some idea of redemption does not enter. As Adorno puts it, 'The only philosophy that can be practiced responsibly in the face of despair is the attempt to contemplate all things as they would present themselves from the standpoint of redemption'. In all, a key way to cultivate philosophical thinking is to believe in the transformation power of questioning. As such, being a philosopher in our century is a courageous, heroic act of self-sacrifice. And as the French poet Lamartine affirms, 'Epochs have their sacrifices, like religions'. Contrary to sacrifices that bind change to violence, philosophical sacrifice depends on rational and moral deeds of freethinking human agents.

Philosophy has been for twenty-six centuries the safeguard of universal moral, spiritual, artistic, and political values. As a consequence, neither religions nor revolutionary ideologies have had any triumphs over the art of philosophical thinking. At the end of the day, for philosophy, there has been no higher authority than freedom of thinking itself. But today, more than ever, philosophy is in danger of oblivion and indifference by a world that finds a taste for the superfluous and mediocrity.

As you can see I deplore mediocrity vehemently because I can even see it in my household and among some of my colleagues. This taste for the superficial and the superfluous will result in a world of arrogant and mediocre characters, who neither know anymore how to think about the world, nor do they give others an institutional possibility to teach it. This is where we stand today as philosophers, young and old.

I apologize to share with you my bitterness. It might come to you as a painful experience. It is certainly one for me. But I believe that being better about the terrible shortcomings of the human race is much better than accepting the rise of insignificance among us. It goes without saying that for a philosopher, heroic and courageous criticism is more valuable than apologetic conformism. I call this a 'philosophical revolt' which is a refusal to accept the absurd injustice of mediocrity. This revolt does not necessarily require machine guns and bombs. It requires the passion of thinking as a nonviolent means of crushing the monster of mediocrity. We need to renounce the concept of humanitarian revolution in favour of a deep commitment to philosophical revolt. This means avoiding moral compromises with a world that undermines philosophical interrogation as a mode of universal emancipation of mankind. Hence, the choice will remain open between submission to the laws and regulations of everyday averageness and a relentless consciousness of revolt. This reminds me of these eternal words of Victor Hugo: 'To be just, whatever the season or suffering; to let justice from within the soul stream forth. This is the true luminosity of man.'

You understand, my dear colleague, the intensity and strength of my words is not to force a personal view or push an argument on you. On the contrary, I want you to take the time to think and to judge these matters for yourself. Now it is high time for me to end this letter and to continue my spiritual journey in philosophy.

Yours truly
R

# Seven

## On the Art of Dying

Tehran, 16 July 2008

My dearest friend,

I am sending you this letter from the country of mirages where I am with my old mother for care and to look after. I have to confess that it is hard to see a parent sick or dying, especially at this age in my life, when I feel that I have to prepare myself for an up close and personal meeting with the angel of death. My mother is ninety-five and weakened by her age, so that she is unable to converse easily, but whenever she can speak, she testifies her willingness to leave the world. I understand her, especially now that I am over seventy myself. It may come to you as a surprise, but life is not always easy. And that is the major reason why we can never conquer life. For, as we advance in years, it becomes more or less clear to us, that behind all our efforts in life there is very little after all. There is a very fine saying of Schopenhauer's to the effect that, 'Our whole life long it is the present, and the present alone, that we actually possess: the only difference is that at the beginning of life we look forward to a long future, and that towards the end we look back upon a long past'. As such, in my young days, I always thought that the world is a glorious place to live in, and as time passed by I eradicated the idea that life has a great deal to offer me. Hence, when I look back at my childhood, I find memories coupled with the unexpected, the momentary, and the fleeting, while with age came regrets, bitterness, and doubts. Accordingly, in the dawn of life, love spreads out its beautiful wings before us, but as years increase, it becomes clear that all love is chimerical in nature, and that pride and vanity alone are real. This agrees with the opinion expressed by La Rochefoucauld: 'True love is like ghosts, which everybody talks about and few have seen.' So, as long as we are young, it is pointless to look for wisdom, and later when we are old, and if there is any degree of consciousness, time and age mock our wisdom. Accordingly, as life goes by and we approach the dusk of life, time rolls so fast that life appears as a hollow nut. So truths appear as disguised falsehoods and triumphs turn into deceptive flatteries. But the most curious fact is that it is also towards the dusk of life that our memories bring us back a light melancholy. As you know well, Kierkegaard calls melancholy 'his most faithful sweetheart'. For Kierkegaard, melancholy is an existential emotion which is accompanied by a sense of world weariness. This is exactly how I see an old age, as a state of 'too much spleen' where you lose your ontological sense of orientation. A young person would continuously seek new challenges and experiences because he/she has not yet come to terms with oneself. This 'existential dizziness' is a typical sign of youth. At old age, however, the dizziness turns into a passionless attitude towards existence. Is it a transfiguration and a metamorphosis or is it simply a loss of one's ontological compass? Kierkegaard uses the word 'transfiguring oneself from within' which I think is the best way to characterize a self-consciousness that accompanies the old age. But this being-for-self is not necessarily wisdom at work, which demands an art of listening to one's inner voice. That is why, contrary to general opinion, learning about life is not an attribute of age. I ask you then what is the use of learning in an old age if an old person's spirit is possessed by a sense of conservatism and conformism? I suppose old people, more than youngsters, try to overcome their fear of death by taking refuge in late-age learning. But as the adage goes, '*Si vis vitam, para mortem*' (If you wish life, prepare for death). But wishing life is not enough; we also need to live life to the fullest, even if we don't believe in the modes and fashions of life that are suggested to us by the spirit of the age. My advice to you would be that you have to live life by your own terms and you have to not worry about what other people think. Follow your own inner voice on the meaning of life without paying too much attention to all the noises around you. Let life reveal itself to you. But you also need to be close and open to life by accepting death as a meditation on the meaning of life. As Spinoza argues, 'A free man thinks about death, but his wisdom is in reflections about life, not death'. In other words, we all think about life by thinking about non-life or death. But a wise person is someone who does not think about death, though thinking is a continuous process of living. As Ortega Y. Gasset says, 'Man is a living problem. Life is a drama, because life is walking along the precipices. It is a struggle with oneself and with the world.' In other words, 'To live is to be outside oneself, to realize oneself'. For Ortega, life is the foundation which needs to be made, to be realized and to be lived. Therefore, self-realization is the ultimate goal of life. Gandhi also describes self-realization as the ultimate goal of life towards which all our activities should lead us. He underlines the fact that, 'There is no other way of self-realization except the way of complete self-abandonment'. This abandonment of the self is not the outcome of volition or action, but a state of silent self-consciousness. According to the teachings of the Buddha in the *Dhammapada*, it is, 'When the wise conquer thoughtlessness by awareness, climbing the terraced heights of wisdom, free from sadness viewing the sad crowd below....'

So, I ask you my young friend, do you want to be part of the sad crowd or you see the courage in you to climb 'the terraced heights of wisdom'? No doubt, you need to find the answer in your inner voice. As for me, I think it is necessary to master the chaotic torrent of life. This is where philosophy can be of a great help, not only because it gives me the wisdom to live and understand life, but because it gives life the necessary wisdom that life itself does not have. Now it is time for me to go and I sit nearby my sick mother and take care of her, while I share her moments of sufferings. Waiting for death is the most painful form of suffering. I wish your generation would learn how to turn such sufferings into hope. But I have my doubts, since we are all human beings and no more than that. This is our tragic destiny.

In friendship
R

# Eight

## On Excellence

London, 5 September 2008

My dearest friend,

I read your last letter with a great deal of passion and interest. As you can see from my letter (mailed from London), I left Tehran after the death of my mother with an oceanic sorrow. I had the feeling that I had lost part of myself. The tragedy of life is not the loss of the dearest ones, but that part of life that is gone with them. Despite all, one is never prepared for the loss of a loved one. I thought the best way for me to get over my sadness and suffering was to strengthen my soul by travelling. Travelling has been the way of my life in the past forty years and I have to confess that I have learnt a great deal through my encounters with other people's cultures. And, so, I feel as if I have been able to feel the junctures of human history and not to be unmindful to the noble spirit of human race. Unfortunately, the average human being does not think this way, just because she finds herself subject to laws or customs of only one nation or one culture. But to live in one culture or under one government does not necessarily make us alien to the blessings of human civilization. Our faith in the vision of fundamental change as mutual understanding among cultures comes along with the spiritual awakening of humanity. Perhaps, the greatest battle for this awakening is the moral daybreak to end the long night of enmity among religions, cultures, and nations. It would be fatal for us to overlook this ethical urgency of the moment and to underestimate the invigorating role of philosophy. Please do not forget that we should forever conduct our philosophical resistance on the high plane of dignity and nonviolence.

I say to you, my young friend and colleague, that in spite of the difficulties and humiliations that philosophy finds itself confronted with, it can hew out of the mountain of ignorance a stone of wisdom. However, it is so disgraceful and pitiful, that philosophers, young and old, have become involved in the ruin of philosophy. They have become spiritually weak, materially greedy, and politically indifferent. The world thinks that they are sincere, but wisdom and excellence have already tested their insincerity.

The notion of 'excellence' might strike some modern ears as quaint, but it seems more desperately necessary than ever before. Human societies continue to exist where there is no excellence; but where excellence is banished, civilization is meaningless, and all that remains is mediocre, one-dimensional, and trivial. There is no sense of community possible without excellence because the quality of people living together is based on the quality of their excellence and their ability to exchange multidimensionally. A competitive society, one that divides people into winners and losers, is one dimensional and breeds the absence of excellence. The Hobbesian man, the man who is a selfish beast who cares for nothing but his own well-being, is not a human in pursuit of excellence, but a brute, as in its pursuit of economic gain it forgoes the intellectual and emotional exchange. Thus, excellence is the midwife of true selfhood. This is the moral ideal with which civilization begins and the one with which it survives. Excellence is the parameter of human dignity and worthiness that Socrates sought when he wanted to find the meanings of truth and freedom. And this excellence, as exceptional as it is rare, is what Spinoza considered as the best life devoted to truth and freedom. He demonstrated with his *Ethica* that excellence can be attained only through wisdom. Searching for this wisdom and safeguarding it in times of crisis is the task that Socrates assigned to the philosophers. Socrates put it in his own words when he insisted that the philosopher is a lover of wisdom and that the wise man is a man in pursuit of excellence. And it is precisely the philosopher who has the task to act truthfully, righteously, and justly.

Today's globalized and technological world has given us many benefits, among which is death of distance and unparalleled increase in velocity of exchange at a global level, erosion of borders and barriers in the hands of the Internet-tech generation has created a dramatic challenge for politic of status quo, individuals finding their power through social network, and monetization of personal information that has given a new dimension to influence of opinion in political arena; however, with that positive change comes a great peril, mediocrity, and populism, where devoid of moral capital, political leaders become the yes-men for the most vocal and influential group. Technology may be the modern religion of mankind, but not everyone trusts its pseudo certainties or derives happiness from it. In *The Spirit of the Laws*, Montesquieu presents the following reflection: 'The political men of Greece who lived under popular government recognized no other force to sustain it than virtue. Those of today speak to us only of manufacturing, commerce, finance, wealth, and even luxury.' With the spread of conformism and mediocrity in our world, the pursuit of excellence has become a singularly singular task. Excellence cannot be power, but it can offer us consolation—not in the sense that it tells us life is good, for that would be a lie, but in the sense that it teaches us the art of questioning our certainties. As Bertrand Russell says, 'In all affairs it's a healthy thing now and then to hang a question mark on the things you have long taken for granted'.

The greatest problems of human beings are their certainties. Every age has its passionate and overwhelming certainty. The Middle Ages was consumed by a certainty in salvation. The Age of Enlightenment was symbolized by a certainty in Reason and Progress. The French and American Revolutions were motivated by a certainty in the rightful and absolute will of men. Later we had the certainty in the work and message of positivistic science, followed by the certainty of nationalistic and totalitarian discourses. And nowadays we have the certainty of being uncertain about everything, with the exception of greed for wealth. Nietzsche had no illusion about these certainties. He knew that, 'Madness is the result not of uncertainty but of certainty'. But in today's world a person who asks questions about greed, power, and complacency is supposedly not a 'clubable' character. He/she belongs to no club. And he/she is no good to be chair of a department, dean of a faculty, or CEO of a company. This is not education. Education, according to William Butler Yeats, 'is not the filling of a pail, but the lighting of a fire'.

Let me end my letter, my young fellow philosopher, by writing few lines on education. What is the priority of education in the twenty-first century? Do professors teach at the university only to end up getting a salary at the end of the month? Do students go to the university only to have a degree and enter the job market? Is learning still a top priority in universities around the world? And, finally, does education help us to live life more meaningfully? These questions need to be in our awareness on a daily basis. With such awareness, we can treat people, nature, and mostly life itself in a more empathic manner. In this light, education by definition is an ethical enterprise. In other words, education is more than a way of being: it is an art of becoming. It is not only a process of nurturing the human soul, as the ancient Greeks understood it through the notion of *paideia*, meaning the acquisition and transmission of excellence, but also what a philosopher like Bertrand Russell defines as 'a certain outlook on life and the world'.

In conclusion, may I repeat that nothing can give your generation more hope and encouragement than your own effort to bring into darkness of stupidity a new light of spirit. Never forget the words of King Solomon: '*Stultorum infinitus est numérus*' (The number of fools is infinite).

With all my best wishes

R

# Nine

## On Truth

New York, 3 October 2008

My dear Rainer,

I hope this letter will find you in good health and spirit. I received and read your last letter with deep emotion. It was beautifully written and I can hardly believe that today you turn twenty-five. I remember well the day of my twenty-fifth birthday. I was living in Paris and my philosophy classmates got me a cake with a phrase on it from Simone de Beauvoir: *Vivre, c'est vieillir, rien de plus* (To live is to grow old, nothing more). But you know, the trick is to grow wiser without growing older. The difficult thing about growing old is to accept it. It is, as Pierre Teilhard de Chardin says, 'like being increasingly penalized for a crime you haven't committed'. But if I may say, you are a philosopher, and a philosopher is someone who is supposed to be in friendship with one's self while being in struggle with one's time. A philosopher is like a tragic hero who frees oneself by a conscious act of will from the unconscious forces of instinct and custom, thus realizing one's true self. What is important here lies in the philosopher's liberating act of will. The philosopher has to make an effort to overcome the static view of being and existing. But I think philosophers should not become prisoners of philosophical doctrines and turn them into ideologies. I see the relation between a philosopher and philosophy like the famous Buddhist parable of the raft. The Buddha compares his teachings to a raft that could be used to cross the river, but should be abandoned when one arrives to the other shore. Philosophy is an art of thinking, not an art of seizing and possessing ideas. So, what does all this mean? Well, it simply means that philosophy begins in wonder, but ends in doubt. Being in doubt is an uncomfortable state of mind, but it is much better than having false certainties or dogmatisms. Bertrand Russell argues that, 'Dogmatism is the greatest of mental obstacles to human happiness'. Why? Because dogmatism spreads ignorance and violence. When we look back at human history, we see that the fate of mankind has been in the hands of violence. Behind the rise and fall of every civilization, there is a story of murder, war, or destruction. But violence which served in making the past is so inadequate to the challenge of the future. We need a new vision of life and a new way of looking at the world which surrounds us. For, the risk and cost of being humans have become too high. Violence does not determine who is right; it only reveals who is wrong. As the Buddha says, 'Hatred is never appeased by hatred in this world. By non-hatred alone is hatred appeased.' Isn't it strange that most of us agree with the Buddha, and yet we cannot apply this precept? I suppose it is because our education neglects to put this teaching into practice. I am sure that you know the famous Buddhist parable on anger. One day the Buddha and a large following of monks and nuns were passing through a village. The Buddha chose a large tree to sit under so the group could rest awhile in its shade out of the heat. He often chose times like these to teach, and so he began to speak. Soon, villagers heard about the visiting teacher and many gathered around to hear him. One surly young man stood to the side, watching, as the crowd grew larger and larger. To him it seemed that there were too many people travelling from the city to his village, and each had something to sell or teach. Impatient with the bulging crowd of monks and villagers, he shouted at the Buddha, 'Go away! You just want to take advantage of us! You teachers come here to say a few pretty words and then ask for food and money!' But the Buddha was unruffled by these insults. He remained calm, exuding a feeling of loving kindness. He politely requested the man to come forward. Then he asked, 'Young sir, if you purchased a lovely gift for someone, but that person did not accept the gift, to whom does the gift then belong?' The odd question took the young man by surprise. 'I guess the gift would still be mine because I was the one who bought it.' 'Exactly so,' replied the Buddha. 'Now, you have just cursed me and been angry with me. But if I do not accept your curses, if I do not get insulted and angry in return, these curses will fall back upon you—the same as the gift returning to its owner.' I repeat here the whole story so that you can get the complete mindfulness of the Buddhist teaching. I think we should understand that Buddhism stands more as a spiritual doctrine than as a religious system like Islam or Christianity. As a matter of fact, I am not the only in the world of philosophy who sees a great analogy between Plato's allegory of the cavern and the Buddhist dynamic conception of liberation from attachment to and desire of the world. Look at how Bertrand Russell talks about the Buddha in his famous *History of Western Philosophy*: 'For my part, I agree with Buddha as I have imagined him. But I do not know how to prove that he is right by any arguments such as can be used in a mathematical or scientific question.' As for me, while I have difficulty to accept the Buddhist concept of nirvana, I do subscribe fully to what Buddhism has to say about the non-permanence of happiness in life. Notice that in the teachings of the Buddha, the word *dukkha* is explicitly underlined not only as pain and suffering, but also as whatever is impermanent. The great realism of the Buddha is to argue that the first thing that is impermanent is life itself. In my previous letters to you, I talked about the two concepts of 'love' and 'happiness', but I never mentioned the concepts of 'immortality' and 'salvation'.

You told me in one of your letters that you grew up in a catholic school and your parents took you to the church. But you never mentioned words like 'faith' or 'belief'. I don't know if you believe in God or not. You might think that this is a wrong question to ask. You are right. I am more inclined theoretically to talk about God as a metaphysical concept. As Kant says, 'We cannot comprehend God; we can only believe in Him'. Religions have tried for centuries to find a well-founded reason for this belief. They have built and destroyed civilizations, created the most sublime and the very inhumane in the name of belief in God, and yet, after more than five thousand years of human history, we are back where we were at the starting point. We are still debating about belief or non-belief. But maybe we should approach the question from another angle. Maybe we should agree with Wittgenstein and say, 'At the core of all well-founded belief lies belief that is unfounded'. And the whole problem with this belief is that it has the capacity to turn into a dogma and prejudice. A God of prejudice and dogma is not a principle of harmony and compassion, but a theologically invented personality who rewards good and punishes evil. I mentioned the word 'compassion' because I think it is the key concept of every spiritual or philosophical quest. Many mystics and philosophers talk about a path to Truth. Actually, there is no such thing as a path to Truth. Truth is a horizon, you move one step closer to it and it moves two steps further away.

All human history is a tragic effort to conquer truth, but if truth is conquered, history comes to an end. So as the history of the world proves, the only historical truth is that what we consider as truths in history are historical perceptions. We are born into a history where human decisions and political events have preceded us and we are each educated as to look upon history as stories that are not ours. But it is worth reminding ourselves of the words 'history' and 'story'. The Greek word *historia* means inquiry and study of the past, but a historian like Polybius talks about the educational experience that is received from what he calls *pragmatike historia*. Therefore, the concern of a historian like Polybius is the practical lesson taught to us by history. He writes:

I think history has a special obligation to record such episodes in the drama of tyche and to pass them on to future generations so that those who come after us may not be wholly ignorant of them and may not be confounded by the sudden and unexpected inroads of these barbarians, but instead, having some appreciation of how short-lived and easily repulsed they are, may stand their ground under attack and do everything in their power not to yield to them in any way....

As we can see, the birth of history writing with Herodotus, Thucydides, and Polybius marks the genesis of political society. For the first time, information about the art of organizing a society is handed on to the next generations, in a way that it exceeded the memory of a society. As such, we can say that every idea changes history, but none so fundamentally as those that change the way we look at history. To this day, history retains its link with the ways past thoughts are reconstructed by our own present. So the question I would like to share with you is history as storytelling.

A historian is essentially a storyteller and as Arendt says in *Truth and Politics*, 'The political function of the storyteller—historian or novelist—is to teach acceptance of things as they are. Out of this acceptance, which can also be called truthfulness, arises the faculty of judgment.' In other words, looking back at history as a way of telling a new story entails going beyond the limitations of narrow, monistic thinking. It is a significant form of resistance that allows individuals to share their perspectives with one another, a way of getting to know more about the construction of a common home in which individuals feel they are part of the world. History as storytelling is, therefore, supremely important, and therefore every human being must be allowed to live by the story which seems true to her. We will learn to live with plurality and diversity once we understand that there is a dimension of hope in sharing the story of our joys and sufferings. The exchange of hope does not diminish; it expands and enlarges our spheres of human possibilities. As you can see, this letter is longer than usual, but I did not have the leisure to make it shorter than it is. Thanks for your understanding.

Always and truly
R

# Ten

## On Mediocrity

Toronto, 21 October 2008

Dearest friend,

I am so sorry to hear that your love life is getting you down at the moment. I am not sure there is any specific advice I can give that will help bring back your hope about love. As I might have told you previously, I have never been very successful in love, though I have always been lucky in friendship. A friend is someone who cares about you without insisting to make you unhappy. Actually, it is not a lack of love, but a lack of friendship that makes our lives miserable. According to Montaigne, 'the arms of friendship are long enough to reach from the one end of the world to the other'. With friends we have long-term memories. With those we love we always have short-term romances and desires. As a matter of fact, the reciprocal and mutual kindness and care that we can find in what the ancient Greeks called *philia* is far more intense than *eros*, which like a flame loses its own being by dreaming on a grand adventure. The very process of friendship involves creating an 'Us' which necessitates preventing from a selfish desire to control others. At a more philosophical level, human beings could and should learn from each other and from other living beings. This is because, assuredly, the human race does not represent the absolute truth. It's time for humanity to become friends with the world. We have been its conqueror for such a long time. It does not come to you as a surprise, if I tell you that mankind's livelihood has devastated the world. But it will certainly come as an astonishment to you if I say that the active participation of humanity in the transformation of its own habits of domination is a sign of a spiritual greatness of mankind. Does this enhance self-respect and dignity for us as human beings? It certainly does, but it also makes us more responsible. But who says responsibility means being responsive to the world and making global capitalism and new technologies more responsive and accountable to their wrong-doings and errors. We should ask global capitalism and new technologies if a perpetual quest for wealth, power, and domination is worthy of endangering the biosphere and the whole human destiny. It seems that we are morally lame and philosophically incapacitated for the crisis that we have created and the world we will leave for the future generations. Where are our Goyas and Gaugins and Mahlers and Messiaens? Where are our Pablo Nerudas and Garcia Lorcas? Are we still capable of thinking music as Olivier Messiaen did only few decades ago? He said, 'I give bird songs to those who dwell in cities and have never heard them, make rhythms for those who know only military marches or jazz, and paint colours for those who see none'. One can make a reasonable claim that the phenomenological journey of human being is primarily a civilizational adventure with an ethical undertaking, or more especially, a quest for excellence. When we look into the history of human civilizations, we will discover one fundamental fact: those which laid the stress on power and violence have passed away. Those which laid their stress on the development of excellence have survived. If history has any lesson to teach us, it is the following: excellence is the end that we have to set before ourselves. It is only through a life in excellence that we can bring together the nations into a fellowship. My argument in this lecture would be to show that a life in excellence is an agency and a transformative force, a lived experience underpinning the dialogue and cross-fertilization of cultures. Hence, to make the world a better place to live in, we must do a better job of ourselves. That is what a life in excellence stands for, and it is that which constitutes the final goal of humanity, when we rise from our present existence to a better life.

The term 'excellence' certainly denotes a harmonious vision of the world that sees all cultures and traditions acknowledging as a common horizon of global responsibility. Therefore, the idea of the excellence is one shared by all civilizations; but the notions of what is the best, vary over a wide range of cultures.

Excellence is certainly an attractive moral and political idea, though it remains hard to define. Excellence has been defined in so many different ways that no consensus has emerged. Ancient Greeks were familiar with the word *arête* which was applied to the gods as well as to men. It would be wrong to translate arête as virtue because virtue refers to a feature of a person's psychology. But the word arête can be described as excellence, or as Plato defines it in the *Republic* as 'the condition of one's soul'. To the modern ear, this may perhaps sound very strange, but central to the general outlook of the Greeks was a concern for excellence. For the Greeks, human excellence in general characterized the *kalos kagathos*, the noble and good man. But this nobility of spirit was considered possible only in the context of the polis, the city state, because it is an ethos that excels towards public virtue. That is why paideia was the education through which excellence was fostered. To the Greeks, the supreme task of man therefore was to discover what human 'excellence' is and to achieve it; and paideia traced the steps of the discovery and the growing process and enrichment of the human ideal. The Greeks believed that excellence breeds excellence. So striving for excellence for its own sake, for truth, beauty, and goodness in the whole educational process, was considered as the only way to produce it. For example, in Homer 'being best' (*aristos*) meant a striving for excellence, a supra-personal ideal pursued without compromise, even at the cost of life itself. In the *Ajax* of Sophocles, we can see the same Homeric note: 'Live best or die best, for the best man/ it must be one or the other.' The stress is on the manner, not merely the matter, of living and dying. Therefore, to be aristos, the 'best', one needs to have 'excellence'. One can say that excellence for the Greeks is more than merely an ethical term. It was above all a quality of character, to be realized in action. This is what Aristotle says in Book II, Chapter 6 of the *Nicomachean Ethics* when he summarizes his account of excellence as 'a determining choice, involving the observance of the mean relative to us....' According to Aristotle, excellence, then, is that condition which best suits humans to perform those activities which are distinctively human. Hence, the best life for a human being involves not solitary or disinterested contemplation of the world, but consideration of the human things, such as the just, the beautiful, and the good. Therefore, for Aristotle, the philosophic life, unconcerned with the human good, cannot recognize itself as a pursuit of excellence for human beings.

In the same manner, Cicero believed that there was no other training than philosophy that was more likely to lead to excellence or more likely to deter from the arrogance that threatened justice. He used the word 'humanitas' to describe the refining or humanizing effects of a broad education in the liberal arts. But 'humanitas' meant more to Cicero than high culture or refined manners. It also implied a loftiness of mind reflected in worthy aspirations and high ideals that prized dignity and moral worth and placed honour and virtue before the pleasures and gain that preoccupied boorish and uneducated minds. It further represented the social spirit that came from a maturation of man's innate sense of fellowship and gentleness, and that extended beyond social graces and good manners and humanism to a broader humaneness and sociability that made possible a secure and civilized way of life in an orderly and harmonious society. Cicero goes so far as to present 'humanitas' as the difference between ill-ordered societies with habits of violence and those where moral idealism had a place and where unity and order prevailed, protected by justice and a concern for peace. Excellence was, therefore, to his mind, a most important force in the creation of a proper political community, and another barrier to the onset of political and moral decline.

Once again we can see that excellence in the minds of the Romans as that of the Greeks has to do with values and ideals rather than the expertness. It was the *summum bonum* of these two civilizations. For the civilization of the high Middle Ages, excellence was sanctity and heroism. The saint and the knight were the ideal types because they both abandoned worldly success and material objects. The emperor Charles V abdicated and entered a monastery. Al-Farabi, the tenth-century Persian philosopher, equated Plato's *Republic* with an idea of the city of excellence as a society which had for goal the education of a philosophic elite. Therefore, what governs and in fact creates the idea of excellence in a society is its vision of reality, that which the society in question considers to possess ethical and practical virtues. Now let us ask the central question: what is our idea of excellence? What do we consider to be the highest good towards which all our daily efforts should in the end direct itself? Certainly we do not find heroism or sanctity among our contemporary values. And yet we do have, as we must, a concept of 'becoming better' that gives vitality and creativity to our lives. How can we think of 'becoming better' without supposing it to be an achievable goal? Aristotle argues that human beings define an ideal life by achieving happiness, and this can be done by living life to its full potential, by having a balance of moral excellence and righteousness in society. Following Aristotle we can say that we would attain excellence if we learn how to live our lives in an ideal way, meaning achieving a balance of moral virtue and righteousness. Hegel would call this a 'learning process' (*Bildung*). For Hegel, bildung, while a formative movement of growth and education, requires undergoing and inhabiting a process of encountering and responding to the other, one that interrupts the stability and integrity of one's knowledge and very being. To use Adorno's words, there is in this process 'a will on the part of the subject to jump over its own shadow'. One might say that this ethical choice making is a particular mode of intensifying a Socratic ethics of ignorance in which learning is haunted by uncertainty and aporia, an alterity immanent to life itself. Within this 'Socratic' ethics of existence, to interrupt the stability and integrity of one's knowledge and very being is, in a sense, to live a life which is made of moral choices. Put differently, excellence is not just an ideal; it is a frame of mind. However, excellence, unlike a utopia, is not a systematic and systemic conception of a far better life achieved by human intelligence and will. Utopia is the life of our dreams made flesh. It is an imagined model waiting to be realized. It is the image of a perfect world. But humanity, as imperfect as it is, cannot live in a perfect world. That is why utopian dynamics have always been imposed views. Excellence, on the contrary, does not seek to impose itself upon others. It is a common horizon of exemplarity for all humans. Excellence is life within life where exemplarity is maintained through individual's commitment to excellence as a noble state of mind. There is no sense of community possible without excellence because the quality of people living together is based on the quality of their excellence. Therefore, excellence is not about enforcement of what is good and what is bad. It is not about being rich and famous, nor is it about political ambitions. It is neither a renunciation of the world nor nostalgia of other worlds. It is the adoption of a noble attitude to life which has always been symbolized by the concept of 'wisdom'. As the Chinese philosopher Lao Tzu says, 'To attain knowledge, add things every day. To attain wisdom, remove things every day.' Socrates put this view in his own words when he insisted that the philosopher is a lover of wisdom and that the wise man is a man in pursuit of excellence. Excellence is the parameter of human dignity and worthiness that Socrates sought when he wanted to find the meanings of truth and freedom. The principal achievement of this experience is to overcome immaturity and to deepen the mind through thinking. As such, the beginning of wisdom is found in thinking critically; by thinking critically we come to the question, and by questioning we may come upon the truth. The art of Socratic questioning is important for the critical thinker because the art of questioning is important to excellence of thought. There is no search for meaning in the face of life's fragility and final-ity without the process of questioning. Human life is not just a random act of living in the present, but also that of living in thought. As such, philosophy has a projective dimension in the lives of human beings in a society. There can be no thought of life without a life of thought. As such, in pursuit of excellence we cannot help asking questions about the meaning of our time and our relation to it. But to do that, one has to expose oneself to what Hannah Arendt calls 'the junction points of life'. Being exposed to the meaning of life is to be gripped by the idea and the passion that life and thought are one. It means simply that one places one's thought at the very corner of one's life and at the same time takes the theme of human life as the main axis of the process of thinking. This process of thinking has always been in relation with the simple fact of being born in a world where life has no other goal than living among others. If thinking and aliveness become one, then certainly one can get to the conclusion that human history is a meaningful process and a significant development of life and thought. Therefore, life is not only something which is 'already there' (*ein vorhandenes*), but something which is 'its own externality toward itself'. In other words, thinking is an opening up to the world which goes hand in hand with acting as the institution and organization of a common world. It is a *kosmos koinos* (common world) in which each of us has his/her own *kosmos idios* (private world). That is to say, it is within the framework of the social-historical institution of the world that one can think and talk. So there is never any possibility of a tabula rasa and therefore the search for the conditions of thinking and acting can never be radical since we think and we act in history and with history. Under these conditions, the primary problem of any moral philosophy is the fact that humans have the potentiality to give their individual and collective life a signification that they have to make. We can interpret this phenomenon as the emergence in society of the possibility and the demand for excellence. We can call this an unavoidable effort at remaining true to the ethical, however precarious and difficult and uncertain. Remaining true to the ethical is to be reminded of a timeless ideal of excellence. It is a defiant act in situation of mediocrity and banality. That is to say the pursuit of excellence is a reciprocal relation to the ethical as a way of relating to truthfulness. Excellence is, hence, a hermeneutic act of remaining true to the ethical while engaging oneself to perceive the spirit of the other in a threefold perspective of mutuality, solidarity, and hospitality. As ethical categories, solidarity, mutuality, and hospitality embody a dialogical function, but also extend a hand of friendship to others as an extension to the spirit which moves within them. Valuing hospitality, mutuality, and solidarity could well act as a necessary antidote to the endemic fears that are the result of the misperception, misunderstanding, and stereotyping of the other. It is interesting that though people have discussed prejudice for centuries, they continue to type and stereotype each other, often perceiving others not merely as being different, but as inferior in their capacity to learn, make decisions, and govern themselves. Therefore, the enemy phenomenon is a powerful excuse for not keeping in tune with the ethical. However, dialogical understanding as true matrix of pursuit of excellence generates a new approach to the phenomenon of civilization as a process of listening and learning. That is to say there can be no process of civilization making without a strong sense of empathy for other human beings as citizens of human history. A feeling of empathy is necessarily a matter of sharing life with others, a recognition of the fact that in the context of human life certain others are similar to us as humans, though different from us as members of another tradition of thought. We can see from this that living in a tradition of thought is automatically accompanied by a sense of shared values with other members of the same community. But it has also to do with what we might call a universal impulse, in the sense that its orientation towards its own life experience is based on an understanding of other communities as different experiences of the same shared life. Civilization is a difficult and daunting task. It is a never-ending quest for excellence and

exemplarity. It is the thin distance that mankind
has placed between itself and barbarism. To learn
to think beyond mediocrity, as an absence of
excellence, we not only have to unsettle and shake
up our well-entrenched concepts and categories,
but our task is also to resist our comfortable and
familiar ethical and political categories which
turn us away from ethical and spiritual definitions
of life and sink us deeper into barbarism. That is
the reason why the pursuit of excellence represents a deep change in our being. It is not simply
standing where we are in our particular world
views and speaking it out to others and listening
to others from afar. It calls for a true ethical challenge and a true responsibility, a willingness to
revise and transform our global culture in a critical and dialogical way. But it also means that this
consciousness of the ethical and this essential
task of mutuality and togetherness is an effort of
making a global ethics across cultures and religions. We should not forget that from the acceptance of mediocrity to barbarism is only one
step. If we wish to resist the tendency of our

civilization towards mediocrity, we need to liberate ourselves from any self-imposed dependency; otherwise we should be prepared to accept barbarism. Let us repeat that the pursuit of excellence is the greatest gift human beings have, but it comes into real life only by taking place among human beings. It is only then that thinking freedom and freedom of thinking can get together. It is not because one has lost freedom of thought that thinking freedom becomes impossible. But there can be no real freedom without a life of the mind. Because thinking life makes life more exciting and a life of thought makes the person conscious about his/her capacity of being free. The Czech philosopher Jan Patocka once wrote, 'A life not willing to sacrifice itself to what makes it meaningful is not worth living'.

So, you see my friend, from my point of view those who believe in life as excellence, life itself is its own excellence. Striving for excellence is a sure way to make our life stand out of mediocrity because excellence is a better teacher than mediocrity. It is a task, not a given. It is the gradual result of always striving to do things in a spirit of nobility and exemplarity. It would be wrong, therefore, to think of excellence as a state of perfection. Perfection is not the only alternative to mediocrity. A more ethical alternative is excellence. When we live in excellence, we might not know what ideal aspect is present in our life, or in the life of another. But we surely know that if there is a pursuit of excellence, it is about living our lives as nobly and as ideally as possible. You'll have to excuse my lengthiness, but I think the subject so well deserved it. I promise you a shorter letter next time I write to you. Try to put away your sorrows and continue to reflect the most confrontational and radical thought of our age. The more I think it over, the more I feel that there is nothing more truly necessary to our times than to think about justice and disobey injustice.

In friendship
R

# Eleven

## On Responsibility

Quito, 17 November 2008

Dear colleague,

I am writing you this letter from the capital of Ecuador. But each time I am back in Latin America, I feel the ontological weight of great writers, poets, and revolutionaries who lived deep and sucked out all the marrow of Latin American life. When we compare the sensual, passionate, and explosive personalities of Latinos with the cold, unpassionate, and indifferent characters of white North Americans, you understand why someone like Che Guevara would say that 'the true revolutionary is guided by great feelings of love'. For Che, life was a daring adventure. For the heroes of modern market societies, life is a shopping trolley. There is nothing more immoral and unpassionate than living in North American safe havens. We think of these safe havens as temples of peace and serenity, while the world is burning in bloodshed and violence. But this is no more than a myopic and self-centred view that has replaced all forms of dialogue and exchange with a culture of conformity and complacency. You can see this absence of dialogue in the culture of stereotype and demonization that give shape to the narrow-mindedness and short-sight judgements of many North Americans. As Michelangelo asserts, 'The greater danger for most of us lies not in setting our aim too high and falling short; but in setting our aim too low, and achieving our mark'. But for those who travel around the world and try to understand other cultures, rather than just laying all day on the beaches in the Caribbean resorts, two things are certain: respect for people of other cultures is better than violence, and people of different traditions can teach us a great deal about history and life. Finally, when there is understanding and cross-cultural friend-ship, trust replaces fear. This is certainly a way for humanity in general to move beyond its infancy.

For too long, Latin America was portrayed as a continent of violence. And needless to say, when we think of violence in Latin America, events such as the Mexican Revolution, the Chilean coup d'état of 1973, the Cuban Revolution, the murder of Archbishop Romero in El Salvador, and so on, come immediately to mind. The fact that these events and many others had to do with the American political, economic, and military involvements in Latin America is deeply troubling. But more troubling is that this violence was done in the name of the supremacy of one culture, notably a lawful, orderly, market-oriented democracy, against what was considered as the rule of undisciplined, uneducated poor masses of Latin America. The paradox here is that the higher the puritan morality, the more vicious the hatred against revolutionaries and righteous individuals who were portrayed as evil. Frankly speaking, I don't see any great political wisdom in killing people in Latin America, Africa, or the Middle East in the name of democracy. History is witness that views and projects that put all the blame on the enemies do not work. But as Shatov declares in Dostoevsky's *The Devils*, 'We are all to blame, we are all to blame ... and if only all were convinced of it'. This opens a new dimension of cosmopolitan mutuality and global co-responsibility.

If we talk about global co-responsibility, then the most urgent political task in today's democracies is to reinvent responsible citizenship. For the past two hundred years the citizen in the West has been only a voter and a consumer of services. In a service society that is hierarchically organized and fragmented along lines of specialization, a citizen is not a public actor. Today, the crisis of politics necessitates the reinvention of an active citizenship. Without active citizenship we cannot be co-creators of history and we will continue to live passively within narrow and ineffective institutions. Thus, the narrow conception of party politics held today limits the role of citizenship in public life. For Aristotle, remember, politics is about developing the virtue of the citizens. Citizenship, then, is the essence of the existence of the political community. The political responsibilities of citizenship could hardly be greater, but for Aristotle the education system must be shaped in such a way to ensure that citizens are capable of attaining the ultimate virtue. As such, the political community requires fully functioning individuals to achieve its ends. In short, the reinvention of citizenship underscores the notion not only that citizens share common purposes and perform actions consistent with those purposes, but also that they develop a feeling of civic friendship. This is more than what Bentham calls 'the interest of the community' which is 'the sum of the interests of the several members who compose it'. From my point of view, membership in a political community requires more than simple presence and having interests in that community. It requires a shared vision and an understanding of civic solidarity. But this civic solidarity fully absorbs the concept of globality. For this very reason, we need to look at the concept of citizenship far beyond the immediate community that one exists in. This underscores the point that while national and ethnic communities need to be protected, we all live on one planet, share its resources, and have a duty to protect it. We get back to our discussion on diversity and the intercultural imperative. Making sense of global citizenship means to increase awareness and promote respect for the many diverse cultures around the globe. This growing awareness of the interconnectedness of our everyday lives with others throughout the world helps us to share our passions of democracy and our different experiences of citizenship. I feel that we need to look at this challenge anew and recognize that we must live together. Today there is no longer a choice between community-based citizenship and global citizenship. It is either responsible global citizenship or non-existence. This simply means that moral solidarity and the recognition that our moral responsibilities do not stop at borders, must come before the political institution of global citizenship. However, what is also true is the fact that there is a growing awareness of the need to go beyond this violence. One can suggest that although violence has come to be accepted as the dominant characteristic of human society in the future, there is also considerable evidence to suggest that nonviolence is a strong element in the refashioning of the human culture. In other words, nonviolence has to be viewed in a new perspective informed by a reappraisal of the new challenges of the future world to it in order to make it more effective. This new perspective and this reappraisal are essentially the functions of education in nonviolence. All this amounts to saying that a new teaching in nonviolence means a whole paradigm shift in the question of civilization. By replacing the notions of 'fundamentalism' and 'nationalism' with that of nonviolence, a new education can be promoted and thus give people correct guidelines for acting for mankind's survival. Gandhi's practice and perfection of nonviolence testified that where challenges and issues manifest themselves on the roadmap of human destiny, humanity has no choice but to continue striving for nonviolence despite the challenges and issues. A change in the guiding principles of human morality is basic to a change in the principles that guide the life of nations. If we are to go beyond nationalism, the way of the future is to think and ask questions about the universality of nonviolence. We just need to remember what Gandhi said: 'I can only say that my own experience in organizing nonviolent action for a half of a century fills me with hope for the future.'

Let me finish this letter by telling you a story. You have certainly heard about the story of blind men describing an elephant to one another. One man feels the trunk and says the elephant is like a snake. Another touches the leg and describes the elephant as being like a pillar. A third puts both hands on the side of the elephant and concludes it is more like a wall. Originally a Hindu, a Persian, or a Buddhist tale, this teaching has been used in many cultures to illustrate that what we all see in our different cultures is only part of the totality. The assumption is that we are all living today a cross-cultural experience that not only challenges, but also completes the experience of modernity in our world. In other words, global civilization has become a plural game of negotiations and interrelationships. There is also an equally important phenomenon: this mosaic-like configuration of the civilization to which we all belong reflects all levels of consciousness. All the cultures of our planet seem to have a say in that matter. This very fact poses the problem of the coexistence and conversation of these cultures. The global world and its challenges are now everywhere because they are interactively constructed everywhere. But they are also in a series where political interactions and cultural symbiosis take place. As far as this play with the meaning and challenges of globalization is concerned, the West is no more the only player in the game, even if the advanced industrial societies in the West have a head start. Each culture discovers oneself in other cultures. As such, no culture can survive without seeing oneself in the mirror of the other cultures.

Therefore, a sense of solidarity is created not only because of the consciousness of similarities, but also because of the dissimilarities and differences that exist between human cultures. In fact, dissimilarities potentially bring every culture to an awareness of solidarity with other cultures. This awareness is not only based on knowledge of the Other, but also on a reciprocal empathy. Dialogue with the Other is a dialogue with the self. In other words, every culture sees the other culture as event and openness. The presence of the other culture is vital for creating new possibilities and so a new horizon of truth is brought forward by the encounter with the other cultures. Therefore, each culture can serve as a corrective to the other cultures. The solidarity that emerges from a dialogue of cultures will always be accompanied with a horizon of a shared life and what we have in common as humans. This general sense of what binds cultures to each other emerges also through an awareness of the particular ways that cultures are bound to each other. It is interesting that this territory of plurality and solidarity can emerge despite ontological and anthropological differences between cultures. Each culture has a specific way of perceiving the world and a particular way of being in time. Not every culture in the world views the concept of time in the same way. Some cultures are wary of time and some ignore the time that passes by. There are cultures (for example, the American culture) which define their way of being in the present and in the future through time. Some (like the Amazon Pirahã tribe) don't have a sense of time in the Western sense of the term. They have no past tense because everything happens in the present. Their culture is a culture of 'carpe diem'. It is interesting to see that even when cultures live in the present with no modern conception of time, the collective experience of the immediacy of time could be translated in a form of dialogue. Human beings are narrative animals and all human cultures have a way of giving an account of what they do. We have no choice but to learn more about each other if we intend to protect our shared values. If we succeed we will be helping to create an era of responsible global politics where intercultural border crossing and learning would replace global mass culture. This is only possible if the concept of trust replaces that of fear and insecurity.

Generally speaking, civilization is not merely the freedom to progress and to advance, but also the ability to ensure that what one chooses is the result of an ethical sense of duty and human solidarity. Humanity cannot be an advanced civilization as long as cruelties, vanities, arrogances, and hypocrisies are predominant on empathies, compassions, and friendships. In other words, civilization, in order to be an ongoing moral progress, has to combine the dynamic and innovative characteristics of the dialogue. Civilization calls for a true ethical challenge and a true responsibility. To learn to think beyond the inhumane, as the absence of the ethical, we not only have to unsettle and shake up our well-entrenched concepts and categories, but also to resist our comfortable familiar ethical and political categories which turn us away from a passionate life of learning and sharing and sink us deeper into mediocrity and provincialism. You are young, however, you can see that our world has changed and has become more and more diverse. This diversity is an essential condition of our global world, which is somehow exemplified by cross-border migrations. Over the last decades, due to the inevitable process of political and social globalization, this phenomenon has reached a considerable size. However, this migration has not led necessarily to a better understanding of shared values and respect for cultural differences, both of which are essential for the future of democratic development in the world. The key here to integrate different cultural and religious minorities is the ability of the society to enable the immigrants to become active members of their new societies. Finally, when assessing diversity, we need to remember that although violence related to diversity is a clear sign of absence of dialogue, it should not be confused with capacities of conviviality and solidarity in different cultures. No cultural tradition or religious belief can serve as 'excuse' for violence, but no state should practice racism and exclusion against cultural traditions and believers of certain religion in the name of democracy. Democracy is also a substantial promise to produce a fair distribution of opportunities for all. In principle, European and North American democracies need to satisfy the generic qualities of any modern political democracy by facilitating access to citizenship and public sphere and removing restrictions on the exercise of individual freedom of those who are lawful residents. It goes without saying that the politics of integration and accommodation needs the adoption of a culture of dialogue which stresses tolerance and embraces the belief that all cultural viewpoints are equally valid in the democratic debate. Following this line of thought we can say that the debate over citizenship and civil rights go hand in hand with that on the moral promise and deliberative virtues of intercultural dialogue. Equalization of citizenship is not only a matter of rights; it is also a matter of mentalities. The basic premise here is the symmetrical encounter between two self-conscious citizens from two different religious and cultural backgrounds recognizing each other as equals.

Today in our world, the unrelenting tide of desperate people fleeing war-torn or unfree homelands to find refuge and better opportunities in Europe and North America has confronted the human consciousness with a new moral issue. More than just being a political aberration, this massive influx of refugees raises a moral question about the nature of human civilization in the second decade of the twenty-first century. Can the West still claim to be civilized when it has undergone a de-civilizing process due to which it has turned into a highly complacent, conformist space of mind where fear, violence, and mostly indifference dominate the everyday life of the Westerners? Given the tragic and inhumane evidence of the new migrations, we can no longer accept the idea of Western moral progress. As history shows us, the everyday meaning of 'civilized' has come to imply the alleged moral superiority of the West vis-à-vis the so-called 'primitive' people, a notion widely used by colonizing nations in the past to ascertain white

supremacy. Whatever moral ascendancy humanity once held has been lost in the refugee camps
around the world where people are treated worse
than animals. The ongoing tragedy of the migrants
raises the general question of the process of 'de-
civilization' in our societies. In his masterwork
*The Civilizing Process*, Norbert Elias describes
this process as a long-term transformation of
interpersonal relations and modes of behaviour
that accompanies the formation of a unified state
capable of monopolizing physical violence and
thus of progressively pacifying society. However,
the migrant crisis can be interpreted in part as the
product of a reversal of these trends, that is, as a
process of de-civilizing whose principal causes
are to be found in the de-pacification of Western
societies where urban violence is becoming more
and more intense, the privatization of politics as
the art of organizing the society accompanied by
the slow erosion of the Western public space and,
finally, the movement of social and political indifference among the European and North American
citizens and the rise of conformism as a general

social attitude in the West. It goes without saying that violence and fear form the Gordian knots of the migration crisis (and they are integral to the moral transformation of the Western societies) which while losing its founding values like compassion and civic friendship, shows strong signs of fear of contamination and degradation via association with inferior beings—the migrants. The shift from classical idea of the communal ghetto to the mental ghetto may be presented dynamically in terms of the interaction of three elements. The first is the relativization of moral values. The contemporary Western society is an increasingly loose domain where no particular moral or ethical position can actually be considered 'right' or 'wrong' and where there is a fairly wide sense of uncertainty. A second element entails the impossibility of meaningfulness in the public sphere and the rise of privatization of morality which makes human beings insensitive and uncompassionate towards the sufferings of others. Finally, the third element of de-civilization which has attained its peak in the Western world is the erosion of the presence through public education. At stake here in the debate surrounding education as a de-civilizing process versus education as valued pedagogy is the notion of critical thinking. The absence of a shared compassion and sense of urgency in the issue of the suffering of the migrants suggests clearly the inability in the Western societies for thinking differently. The hubris of Western democracies towards the massive humanitarian disaster caused by the migration crisis is to stick to its 'democratic values' and all will be well. But the self-congratulatory claims to universalism of Western democracies seem to have destroyed the sense of empathy in the Western world. The world of sufferings and tragedies of the migrants that the West is witnessing is as remote from the present Western mind as the farthest of the planets. It is this uncompassionate remoteness which makes things even more tragic.

So my friend, what can a philosopher do about all these tragedies, except to write about them and try to share his or her concerns with an indifferent world. Admit it or not, at the bottom of all our problems in today's world, lies the problem of indifference. And I fully agree with Iris Murdoch that, 'Perhaps misguided moral passion is better than confused indifference'. It's time for me to end this letter and to have a drink of guarapo with my Ecuadorian friends.

Thinking the best for you

R

# Twelve

## On Patriotism

Barcelona, 23 November 2008

My dear Rainer,

From time to time I get wind of your beautiful mind through your letters. Thank you very much for your letters. I have asked my secretary to separate your letters from those of my colleagues and friends, so that I spend more of my spare time responding to yours. Those of us who are writers and not solely educators may perhaps draw some hope and comfort by imagining that our writings will remain alive and accessible to others long after we are gone.

However, my dear friend, philosophers need to remain immune from the notion of posterity; otherwise the value and sensibility of their thought would turn into conditioned reflexes. As Adorno points out magnificently, 'The hope of leaving behind messages in bottles on the flood of barbarism ... [is] an amiable illusion'. Thinking can easily choke up with celebrity. Therefore, it is a necessity for philosophers to remain detached, while trying to live life fully and to bring the intensity of life into their works. This intensity is what should remain when decades from now people will read our words. The excellence of every philosophical thought is its intensity, capable of making all immaturity and infantilism evaporate. Though, as with the recounting of a dream, words seem lame once put on paper. We might consider it natural if young readers like you retained words from the philosophical or literary texts they cared about. Our conscious mind can lie down when and where it pleases. But the past is not a place to dwell; otherwise it will turn into nostalgia. A nostalgia that comes to us has duration in time, but has no weight and no texture in reality. We read the poets and philosophers of the past, but we live them in the present. Kierkegaard expressed a central truth when he said, 'Life is lived forward, but it is understood backward'. This is a saying with staying power because it remains capable of being re-thought and reinvented.

Despite the juggernaut of global technology that has transformed our lives, we still continue understanding life backward. Life is a priceless substance. In comparison to it all wealth of this world is temporary. We don't just have the right, we have the duty to defend the principle of life against arbitrary power and against cynicism. You can maintain your substantial position on the principle of life silently and constantly, but you need to shout it out philosophically without abandoning it. Moreover, life is a silent partner, of whom you can never predict when she will abandon you with the striking bell of death. 'For in that sleep of death what dreams may come,' as

Shakespeare writes in *Hamlet* (Act 3, Scene 1). But I don't know how to hate death, my own death. Yet, I despise the death of my beloveds. Maybe because we never live our own deaths. Others die with us and for us, and we die with others and for others, but we never die for ourselves. 'The life of the dead,' affirms Cicero, 'is placed in the memory of the living'.

Most surprisingly, the once well-defined dividing line between life and death which was thought by religions appears, in our times, to becoming shadowy and fuzzy. Don't you think it's strange that the technological capacities of human civilization in the contemporary world have given her so little ability to understand death without being indifferent to it? If a medieval man were to think death, he would probably think it simply in relation to his fear or love of God. To a medieval man, God was eternal and so was life after death. From the point of view of many religions, we cannot die, because death is actually imposed on us by God as the death of our body. As such, death and eternal life are achieved by the mercy of God. In this

realm of consciousness, we can find no meaning
to life and death outside the presence of God. But
for us who have made such great steps in science
in the absence of God, for us who consider faith as
unacceptable to the rational mind, for us human
creatures caught in the riddle of the present time,
how can we deal with the meaning of death?

'A man's determination to become beautiful is
always a desire for death,' says Yukio Mishima.
What really interests Mishima is not life, but
death. It is in the act of confronting death that
the sense of beauty reveals itself. Rilke, one of
Mishima's favourite poets writes, 'For beauty is
only the beginning of a terror we can just barely
endure, and what we so admire is its calm disdain-
ing to destroy us'. Rilke underscores omnipres-
ence of beauty next to the immanence of death.
He departs from the premise that we humans have
fashioned beauty in order to make sense of the
destructive force of death. Death, this permanent
existential threat, is turned into a transcendent
event far from the life we inhabit. That is why
Rilke adds, 'Death is the side of life that is turned

away from, and unillumined by us'. But whether as a transcendent event or a life-affirming experience, death is more than a simple biological fact for humans. We, humans, have horror of death, but we are the only beings that can choose the time and space of our death.

In the autumn of 1960, Yukio Mishima wrote a short story entitled 'Patriotism', which he later turned into a short film. The story describes in detail the heroic double suicide of Lieutenant Shinji Takeyama and his wife Reiko. On 25 November 1970, Mishima ceremoniously disembowelled himself after addressing the Jieitai soldiers at the Eastern Army Headquarters in Tokyo. The similarity between the heroic seppuku of the young lieutenant in 'Patriotism' and Mishima's own death is breathtaking. Mishima's portrayal of this death is a brief but masterful piece of prose:

By the time the lieutenant had at last drawn the sword across to the right side of his stomach, the blade was already cutting shallow and had revealed its naked tip, slippery with blood and grease. But, suddenly stricken by a fit of vomiting, the lieutenant cried out hoarsely.

The vomiting made the fierce pain fiercer still, and the stomach, which had thus far remained firm and compact, now abruptly heaved, opening wide its wound, and the entrails burst through, as if the wound too were vomiting. Seemingly ignorant of their master's suffering, the entrails gave an impression of robust health and almost disagreeable vitality as they slipped smoothly out and spilled over into the crotch. The lieutenant's head drooped, his shoulders heaved, his eyes opened to narrow slits, and a thin trickle of saliva dribbled from his mouth. The gold markings on his epaulets caught the light and glinted.

Blood was scattered everywhere. The lieutenant was soaked in it to his knees, and he sat now in a crumpled and listless posture, one hand on the floor. A raw smell filled the room. The lieutenant, his head drooping, retched repeatedly, and the movement showed vividly in his shoulders. The blade of the sword, now pushed back by the entrails and exposed to its tip, was still in the lieutenant's right hand.

It would be difficult to imagine a more heroic sight than that of the lieutenant at this moment, as he mustered his strength and flung back his head. The movement was performed with sudden violence, and the back of his head struck with a sharp crack against the alcove pillar. Reiko had been sitting until now with her

Letters to a Young Philosopher

face lowered, gazing in fascination at the tide of blood advancing toward her knees, but the sound took her by surprise and she looked up.

The lieutenant's face was not the face of a living man. The eyes were hollow, the skin parched, the once so lustrous cheeks and lips the colour of dried mud. The right hand alone was moving. Laboriously gripping the sword, it hovered shakily in the air like the hand of a marionette and strove to direct the point at the base of the lieutenant's throat. Reiko watched her husband make this last, most heart-rending, futile exertion. Glistening with blood and grease, the point was thrust at the throat again and again. And each time it missed its aim. The strength to guide it was no longer there. The straying point struck the collar and the collar badges. Although its hooks had been unfastened, the stiff military collar had closed together again and was protecting the throat.

Please forgive me for quoting such a long paragraph from Mishima's book, but I think the grandiose writing of this unjustly underestimated author is worth long citations. Mishima teaches us the beauty of death because death can become an ideal, as it is the case for the Samurai. The heroic death is the culmination of life. It is a pure death, free from boredom, sickness, and mediocrity. As Mishima says, 'To choose the place where one dies is also the greatest joy in life'. This choice represents the dignity of Man, but also the dignity of death. That is why Holderlin affirms in *The Death of Empedocles*: 'For death is what I seek. It is my right.' In today's world, death is medicalized and by the same token de-aestheticized. We live like dogs, serving masters that throw us bones, and we die like rats, meaningless, abandoned, and forgotten. Death is the absolute beyond which nothing is meaningful. Therefore, a philosopher needs to give meaning to his death. This is what Socrates does by choosing his death as an apogee of his philosophical thinking. Socrates's suicide is the greatest victory of philosophy against the banality of human mind and action. What Jacques-Louis David's *The Death of Socrates* reveals to us is the philosophical integrity of the philosopher at the moment of taking his own life. Socrates chooses to die not because Athenians want him to die, or because his disciples want him to escape from prison, but because his *daimon*, the philosopher's divine inner voice, tells him the time and place of his heroic death. In David's painting, Socrates is speaking while he is reaching for his death cup. This is the great gesture of philosophy to death revealing its commitment to excellence in life.

I apologize for this long letter, which might seem to you as burning with a feverish passion of words. Let's hope we shall meet very soon and share together moments of philosophical drunkenness. By the time this letter reaches you, I will be travelling again and most probably reading you on my return.

In friendship
R

# Thirteen

## On Democracy

Delhi, 28 December 2008

Dear Rainer,

This time I decided to write to you on my birthday. Jean Paul wrote, 'Our birthdays are feathers in the broad wing of time'. Life is not right in all cases, but at the end one is grateful for little things in life. Believe me I care for your letters in the same way as a child for his toy. I read and read again all your letters and try to feel them as sincerely as I can. You can't imagine how thrilled I am when I return home from my travels and lectures around the world and find your letter sitting on my desk by the grace of my secretary.

I am awfully glad to hear that you have started working on your book about freedom. Freedom is the most precious idea in the possession of human beings, and yet they waste it like they waste time. We waste more time in arguing what freedom is than by thinking freely. Freedom lost is freedom we have not thought. It is freedom left empty. We cannot learn the secret of freedom because freedom has no secret. Many among us moderns consider freedom as non-interference. To the Romans, it meant being a citizen and not a slave. How ironical that we the modern citizens of liberal societies find ourselves as living in freedom under regimes of law and yet we have no consciousness of this law which is the source of our liberty. We could consider this as our democratic weakness. Unfortunately, the promise of democracy has not strengthened and heightened the consciousness of freedom and the sense of responsibility among the citizens of liberal societies. Democracy, by pandering to the indifference of people, has degraded both itself and the people. So, democracy alone will never be enough. Democracy cannot be established through elections and a constitution. Something more is necessary. What is needed is an endless stress on democracy as a practice of moral thinking and moral judgement. In other words, we can never build or sustain democratic institutions if they do not have a goal to help us become more humane. But more than that, it means having a Socratic experience of politics as self-examination and dialogical exchange. It is the admission of ignorance in us, and the recognition of ignorance in others that gives democratic spirit the courage to be a true confrontation with an open century which contains an awareness both of the complexity of the issue and of the fundamental importance of pursuing a solution. If, through a Socratic experience, every citizen can be drawn out of the simple mechanism of voting and engaged in a more responsive and more responsible process of self-government and self-structuring of the society, we might see the beginnings of a healthy return to democracy. So long as we believe that democracy is only a marketplace depending on fair and voluntary economic and political exchanges with a stable legal system, we cannot build a democracy even though we may defend public liberties.

But the fate of democracy is interrelated to our own fate. After all, democracy is made by humans and has its fate related to the human condition. Though the human condition is such that we can never be certain about the positive result of our actions, we can never take forward a nonviolent democracy if we ignore our responsibilities and deny that there in these strange years after the end of history and on a planet overheating by violence and environmental damages, it is possible to strive for democracy because it is possible to remain true to the ethical. Gandhi saw personal transformation, political action, and constructive programme as intertwined, all equally necessary to achieve social change. But Gandhi was aware of two great dangers to nonviolence and peace in human societies—national egotism and religious fanaticism. That is why he announced that intolerance is the worst of violence and he encouraged a dialogue among cultures and religions. He once said, 'I do not want my house to be walled in on sides and my windows to be stuffed. I want the cultures of all the lands to be blown about my house as freely as possible. But I refuse to be blown off my feet by any.' This is the statement of a person who aspires for openness and integrity in life.

If I can give you only one advice, it would be to leave yourself open to other insights. Let your inner life take you to new frontiers where everything is creating and understanding. And then you will have your time of intellectual incubation and philosophical gestation. Being a philosopher means ripening like a tree, but not any kind of tree. It is being like an oak tree which fears no storms and stands firm through troubles and dangers. The more time and trouble the oak tree confronts, the stronger it gets! But it remains humble and always in a gentle mood. Philosophers need to learn humility from the oak tree. As Saint Augustine affirms, 'It was pride that changed angels into devils; it is humility that makes men as angels'.

Finally, to end this letter, I would like best to write few words about empathy. As I have mentioned before elsewhere, empathy is an essential component of ethical citizenship and solidarity with another person. It is our ability to be part of a plural world. From this perspective, empathy is an emotional force which can produce a dialogical receptivity and reciprocity among the citizens. It is a political art through which we come not only to know and understand the other, but also to respond to the other ethically which calls for an ethics that emphasizes the imperatives of mutual learning among cultures. This brings us to see in humanity a permanent challenge and a continuous process of questioning of our certainties. Therefore, it is not something which annuls plurality and multiplicity of traditions and cultures through an arrogant affirmation of one culture on others. On the contrary, humanity is plural in essence because it is a permanent questioning of any self-satisfied manifestation of a given view or culture. This is a kind of permanent faith in the dialogic capacities of mankind in forming cultural alliances and building civilizational solidarities. Never forget that nationalism is a danger not only because it is a form of exclusiveness, but because it is an absence of freedom of mind. Therefore, never forsake humanity for nationalism because human solidarity is the highest spiritual vision of mankind. With wishes and greetings.

Yours
R

# Fourteen

## On Herd Mentality

Tokyo, 5 February 2009

Dear Rainer,

I read your last letter with a passionate eye and a heart full of friendship. I have to confess that your letters have added a beautiful colour to my gloomy existence. However, let me say with no hesitation that it is neither my desire, nor is it the time for me at this old age to be impatient about things in life. It has been said and repeated day after day that 'patience is a cure for all sores'. Perhaps this is so, though there are sorrows of heart and diseases of mind that you can never cure, either with patience or with impatience. Unfortunately, this is a Schopenhauerian lesson that I learnt from life.

Talking about Schopenhauer, I am happy that you enjoy reading this great philosopher. I remember the feeling of euphoria I felt the first time I read him when I was eighteen. It was a philosophical pathos approaching a degree of madness. The joy of suddenly discovering an unknown truth (at least unknown to me at the time) hit me like a Midwest lightning bolt. So, I perfectly understand your feeling. Rare are philosophers who can write today with such a conceptual strength and clarity of mind. Moreover, our situation as philosophers is more difficult than at the time of Kant, Hegel, and Schopenhauer. Today our heads are in the hyena's mouth and we must get them out the best way we can by interrogating in the most critical manner our world. If we attempted this, the odds would be against us as they have always been. To fight against the insignificance and the general conformism of our time is as difficult as it is to sit in London and fight with the monarchy.

But I can assure you that as history of philosophy shows us, philosophers do not practice the art of spitting in the wind. We might be considered as mad people by those who totally ignore what madness is, but at least our madness is creative, emancipative, and nonviolent. There are those of us who believe that our contemporary world is suffering from another form of madness which is anti-philosophical and destructive. It is true, a great many simple-minded people have been induced to accept this form of madness as a way of seeking business without preventing a pending evil to choke the fountain of human wisdom once for all. The war that has been waged on philosophy by the Anglo-American tradition of analytic thought has opened our eyes and caused us to form alliances with religion, art, and political theory. Perhaps many scholars and students do not care about what we think and how we feel on this subject. Maybe all those practitioners of positivism or analytic philosophy think of themselves as the wisest and the most pragmatic thinkers of our century. But appearances are deceitful. It is not because they find more jobs and have better budget plans that they are necessarily better philosophers. Remember the case of Schopenhauer and his failures in teaching at the University of Berlin. And yet in two hundred years from now, we will continue reading Schopenhauer while all these so-called 'philosophers' will find themselves among the white pages of history.

You asked me about metaphysics in your previous letter. I think metaphysics is to philosophy what harmony is to music. In the hour of thinking, we cannot do without it. However, at present it looks like philosophy has become the most ignorant and the feeblest of all sciences. But you may rest assured that for those who want to change the pace of today's world, philosophy comes as the chief cornerstone of all forms of transformation and transcendence. This cornerstone should be built into the edifice of comprehensiveness and understanding. Without this our world cannot dedicate itself to thinking freedom and creating free institutions. I must confess it is somewhat embarrassing for us thinkers, living twenty-six centuries after Socrates and Plato, to still urge the philosophical against prejudice and slavery of the mind. There is a herd propensity in the human mind that delights in following a crowd, and in the gratification of this mode of being, it always oppresses another conscience. Let me call your attention to the point that more human beings have herd mentality, more prejudice and violence exist in their hearts and minds. It matters not how much humans may differ upon the questions of customs and mores, but it matters that a group or a nation with a feeble mind look down upon others with a kind of royal distinction. This is a gross and monstrous abomination which has been grafted into the stock of our social life. And when I think of the sad condition of human beings who widely and continuously imprison themselves in this sheep mentality, I feel it a duty and a privilege as a philosopher to set forth the refined legacies of human civilization embedded and gratified by the qualities of philosophical thinking.

Many believe wrongly that the dangers of herd mentality go hand-in-hand with the rise of criminal politics or totalitarian ideologies. The truth is that human civilization has found itself quite often with living examples of racial hatred, national violence, religious terrorism, and ideological barbarity. The lust for power and the *Führerprinzip* are not matters of the past. They can still excite millions of people around the planet to think of themselves as a 'master race' and find natural to put into peril the freedom of others. These are the sinister characters that we encounter in our everyday lives and who fulfil humanity's dark side. Therefore, the evil that we seek to understand and to fight is calculated and devastating, though it is invisible most of the time. Remember what Baudelaire said, 'The attractiveness of the horrific only intoxicates the strongest'. And many years later André Breton, the architect of surrealism added, 'If I obeyed the fiercest and most frequent impulses I feel inside, I would have to walk out into the street with guns in my hands and see what would happen'. This is how the radical evil can come to the surface from the underworld, as it did in 1933 with Hitler. For

Hitler, the radical evil was a given, not a possibility. What he made possible was the massacre of millions of Jews, gypsies, homosexuals, and those who resisted to his conquests. This is what evil is like when it conquers the political space of human beings. It turns the public space into a nursery and the citizens into immature individuals who are incapable of thinking and acting.

This is where the task of philosophy and the responsibility of philosophers start. Their task is certainly not to admire 'the beautiful hands' of dictators and mass murderers or to collaborate or ignore with them. But to fight them, if necessary, with more than philosophical teachings and writings. However, one needs to prepare the civilization of tomorrow and this is where the real task of philosophy resides. Philosophy has always been on the side of what Kant and Fichte call *Die Bestimmung des Menschen* (The Vocation of Human Being). This vocation needs to be renewed at each age and it is the grave responsibility of philosophers to do so. It is important to bear in mind that the basic job of a philosopher is to serve truth, which is to serve life. Life is the only sacred thing in our lives. I speak of this because, looking at the state of our world, I cannot avoid the thought that many people around the world still understand little the close relation between life and truth. The Czech philosopher, Jan Patocka, once said that, 'Life not willing to sacrifice itself to what makes it meaningful is not worth living'.

In friendship
R

# Fifteen

## On the Art of Making Films

Irvine, California, 3 April 2009

My Dear R,

It has been three weeks, I believe, since I received your last letter. Why the delay in answering it? I suppose you guess that I have been travelling again. I wished that was the case. I was actually very sick and so weak that I could barely read or write. I hate watching television, which I think is a great brainwashing machine. But I love watching classical movies. As the French filmmaker Robert Bresson would say, 'Cinematography is writing with images in movement and with sounds'. It is not only bringing the images together that makes cinema an art par excellence. The transcendental meaning of cinema resides in the distance that exists between the camera and reality. As such, being entertained by a movie is one thing, but encountering it as a narrative is another.

The last two weeks I watched a great number of French films. I like very much the films directed by Marcel Pagnol and based on his own writings. I suggest that you watch the great performance of actors like Raimu and Fernandel. This is what we miss the most in today's cinema. In a completely different context, I also like the Cinema Noir, both French and American. I have my favourites, like *The White Heat* with James Cagney, or Anthony Mann's *Raw Deal*, or *Night and the City* by Jules Dassin. Anybody aware of living in the spearhead of modernity hears much talk about the history-making role of cinema. In other words, after more than hundred years of existence, cinema has become the 'lingua franca' of our modernity. Some people like to describe

131

this fact by speaking of Man as essentially a cinematic being and that therefore the riddle of what he is may be unfolded in the image that he gives of himself and his world. As such, the civilization of the twenty-first century believes that Man is finally understandable as a cinematic being.

But how can we write about the cinematic as an animator of our existence without trying to explicate cinema as a mode of thinking. For the simple reason that cinema makes us think. Yet that which is there as an image in the film is also a dynamism related to our self-consciousness as a developing history of meaning. Though cinema may not be meaningful for everyone and at every time, it places upon each one of us the whole burden of meaning. This statement could only be substantiated by a careful analysis of what we are thinking when we think cinema as meaning. In this sense, the act of creation itself is placed upon us as way of making meaning. Meaning, here, is not actually in what we see, that is, the images of cinema, but in the process of thinking that we can bring out of these images. To put the matter simply, any appeal to the process of giving meaning to images must be within a full recognition of the process of thinking.

To use a Nietzschean idea, cinema is the point where 'the philosopher's conviction appears on stage'. Indeed, we have here the very idea of thinking as 'the moving image of eternity'. Yet having said this, I must state that this mode of thinking with images is a moral height for men, and unlike what we might think, it cannot be cheaply bought. This means that at any time or place, human beings can be opened to the process of thinking for themselves through their encounter with the seventh art. What is more beautiful is that cinema is a mode of thinking that can provide us with a condition for productive public conversation.

How does all this go together? In the first place, as I have already mentioned in my previous letters, we need to learn to think for ourselves. We must always stand ready to question the authority of Others, be there political, religious, or simply rational and discursive. If we fail to do so, we are willingly responsible for our own manipulation by Others. In order to not be manipulated and to go beyond all dogmas, we need to use our reason, as Kant says, 'in broad daylight' and not in the shadow corner of the private life. This is why the contrast between *sensus privates* (a private sense) and *sensus communis* (a communal sense) gives meaning to our judgements and experiences as human beings. Have you ever realized to what extent our world is a privatized world? We understand this better when we go back to the Latin root of the word 'private' which means 'deprived' and 'set apart'. What we lack the most in our private realm, with all the security and rights that we believe should stay in the private space, is a sense of common humanity. This is what misses in Benjamin Constant's complete exaltation of modern liberty as the primacy of individual privacy and independence. Though Constant puts in balance the enjoyment of individual interest and the practice of political liberty, he is not concerned as Kant or Hegel with 'a society of world citizens'.

Our world has even stepped further than Constant and talks about 'a society of world consumers'. No wonder why the ideal type of our contemporary society is the 'tourist' and not the 'flâneur'. Walter Benjamin, a great philosopher who left us early in life, talks about the flâneur in his seminal work *The Arcades Project*, as a person who is a 'virtuoso of empathy' because he leads us to a moment at which the past and the present recognize each other. As such, through the art of flânerie the memory of the heritage of the past is rescued in order to understand the present. The flâneur walks through the city listening to its pulse, while the tourist travels the city on a special bus and rushes through its streets and museums. The tourist has neither empathy for the spirits who have lived in these spaces, nor a memory of his own visit in different cities. She ends up in a mall where the great consuming orgy of capitalism takes place. Another point, the tourist does not think. She only knows how to take pleasure from her mercantile orgasm.

I hope it is beginning to become clear for you that such a historical figure like the tourist does not have a great deal of respect for the act of thinking. The tourist can neither think in accord with herself, nor can she think in the position of everyone else. Given this context, it seems clear that the universalization process of the tourist means simply the end of thinking in our world. However, let us pray that any community with a responsible view of itself would not abandon reasoning and drift towards an insignificant life. This brings me, finally, to your question of how we should defend a life in excellence, and more especially in a society in which the distinction between truth and non-truth is not sharp any more. To which the shortest answer is, we defend truth best by living in excellence. Let me close this letter with a stronger claim, that excellence properly conceived and lived helps us to distinguish between critical thinking and arbitrariness, in order to capture the responsibility that we each take for thinking the world. This last style of argument brings us to the possibility that thinking against arbitrariness and complacency of our world could be a central value to the very cultures and cultivated citizens of our world that are striving to survive what remains of our human heritage.

For ever
R

# Sixteen

## On Aesthetics

Toronto, 1 June 2009

Dear friend,

Thank you for your letter dated 1 May 2009. Unfortunately, I do not have all the strength of my previous weeks to answer fully and promptly to your letters. My health is deteriorating rapidly and I have been confined to bed. Let me just say that your letters have brightened my life and made me full of joy and hope. Halfway through reading one of your recent letters, I was overwhelmed with nostalgia for times gone by. It was one of those longing feelings that made me close my eyes and listen to Gustav Mahler's *Kindertotenlieder*. The music transported me back to my times as a student in Paris. I listened to Mahler's great work with the diamond voice of Kathleen Battle. I had the chance to follow Mahler's complete oeuvre at Théâtre du Châtelet. What a nobility of spirit and a delightful practice of high culture. You know, I never gave up on my allegiance to my professors and friends in France; neither did I give up my love of the French language. Though I am now writing you these letters in English, a language which is badly spoken and awfully written, I still feel at 'home' with the French language. Yes, reading your letters and going through the references you make to Albert Camus and Jean-Paul Sartre compelled me, with closed eyes, to revisit some of the finer moments of my student years in France. So, I went to my bookshelf, pulled out Sartre's *Les mots* and Camus's *L'Homme révolté* and began to read passages from each. I found these words of Sartre, which I had underlined: 'One writes for one's neighbours or for God. I decided to write for God with the purpose of saving my neighbours. I wanted gratitude and not readers.' But Camus's perspective in *L'Homme révolté* is very different from Sartre. He says, 'The future is the only transcendental value for men without God'. Considering these two positions, we can ask ourselves why do we write? Why do we write letters? Why do we write books? Why do we write film scripts? And why do we write poetry? To find gratitude or to have a future? Or, to find fame and gratitude through time? But, above all, does writing help us to live a meaningful life?

The aesthetics of writing is subordinated to the ethical process of creating. That is why writing could be considered as an education in virtue and excellence (what the Greeks called arête). Of course, we should be able to distinguish here between calculative writing and meditative writing. This is what distinguishes the work of an author, measured by the force of the soul, from a writing which is measured by the standard of sale and celebrity. Let us not forget that a meditative writing is a way of conducting ourselves in thought (what the German philosophers call *Denkunsgart*). To this end, the difference between Dostoevsky's *The Brother Karamazov* and *Harry Potter* is that the first form of writing brings humanity to a state of philosophical awareness and critical consciousness, while the second fails to help us in asking moral and philosophical questions about the destiny of humanity. That is to say, you don't think with *Harry Potter*, though you might get fully entertained. In it is this context that the works of Sartre and Camus make more sense to us because they coincide with the process of self-knowing that is so central to the ontological vocation of mankind. As a result, the main purpose of writing is to engender a certain ability of spirit in human beings and to incite them to understand and transform reality. We need to keep in mind that authors like Sartre and Camus did not write to be rewarded. They wrote in order to give a meaning to their lives and to the lives of others. This is what writing is all for.

This brings me back to your letter and your demand to meet with me. Be sure that nothing more would make me happy. However, my feeble health does not permit me this joy at the moment. I didn't want to alarm you, but during my last trip to the US, I had a heart attack and I had to visit the hospital. By the way, hospitals resemble more and more of factories of delayed death. The only thing that you don't see at hospitals is a philosophy of life. I suppose doctors and nurses don't have time to think about philosophy. They leave the art of philosophizing to scholars and academics at our universities. But in case you have to pass by a hospital, look more attentively at the entrance and you will see a homeless beggar in torn clothes sleeping on the ground and people who go in and come out pay no attention to him. This beggar symbolizes life itself which is left outside these death-delaying factories. Isn't it strange that life is no more exalted by those who are going to visit a dying person or to die themselves in a solitary way on a hospital bed? Destiny which had for so long been shown to us by a homeless beggar in torn clothes is now in the hands of medical technology. Our familiarity with technology has made us to abandon the familiar idea of our own death.

Best wishes
R

# Posthumous Letter

Dear Mr Rainer,

It saddens me to inform you that Professor R passed away yesterday from complications due to his heart failure. Though he lost his battle against his dreaded illness, he did not suffer much before leaving this world. Since I am the last person who saw him alive, I can assure you that there seemed to be something on his mind in regard with the letters that he wrote you during the past two years of his life. In the months before he died, he asked me to send you this letter accompanied with an old copy of Dante's *Divine Comedy*. As you can see this is an annotated copy with Professor R's handwriting. If you can go to Canto 20 of *Paradiso*, you will see a poem underlined by him. It is written:

*So, while it spake, do I remember me*
*That I beheld both of those blessed lights,*
*Even as the winking of the eyes concords,*
*Moving unto the words their little flames.*

During the last hours of his life he asked me to read this passage to him. There is so much I want to tell you about the last day of Professor R's life, but I do not have the courage to put them into words. During the last two weeks, I gave him almost daily an opportunity to speak to me about his favourite subjects which were philosophy and education. He said:

Patricia, education, the adage goes, is the art of moulding human beings into socialized beings. This will ring true to anyone who has been educated or understands what education is. The socialization can prove effective in turning children into creatures that would obey us without asking any questions. But it should also draw attention to the shortcomings of our present societies where the ideas of morally enlightened and self-sustained individuals are totally absent from the educational projects of humanity. Those now advocating and practicing the private ownership of universities around the world might not care about the spiritually enlightened lives of our forefathers and their heritage for human civilization, but they will come to regret in few decades from now when ceaseless laissez-faire, exploitation, and complacency will turn over our societies into spiritless labour camps. In one word, the extreme concentration of wealth and power has destroyed the roots of moral progress. No less important would be its harmful consequences for the political autonomy and self-creative capacities of our future generations. It follows, therefore, that philosophers like yourself, who are young and full of hope, should be self-educated and self-trained, next to the lesser education that you get at our universities in order to be able to confront and to change the harmful modus operandi of Western society. This would require not only stamping out the economic and political domination, but also emancipating all forms of philosophical, artistic, and spiritual creations from the tutelage of capitalist institutions. These propositions are in no way idealistic. On the contrary, they are pragmatic solutions to the meaningless role of education in our world. As a matter of fact, any future society needs to be supported by these bedrock principles. So the sooner you start your own process of enlightenment, the better. Perhaps the most important component of this enlightenment involves a systematic return to the classics. My central complaint is that members of your generation and those younger than you have turned away from their master thinkers. We must stop turning away from those who can guide us to the future. For the simple reason that they represent the cultural lighthouses of our civilization. Without them we are definitely lost.

As you can see, I am trying to put into several constructed phrases what he murmured to me in his voice of satin. He tried to write to you one last letter, but he didn't have the strength. He was fully aware of going gently into that good night, as the poet says. It is strange, now that I think; he liked very much this poem of Dylan Thomas:

*Do not go gentle into that good night,*
*Old age should burn and rave at close of day;*
*Rage, rage against the dying of the light.*

At last, his breathing became slower and slower and slower, and suddenly it stopped. He remained serene in his dying as he had been in his life. But I am left with rage.

His last wish was to see you become a great thinker with an independent mind. Philosophy was his consolation and it must eventually be yours. Eventually, too, you must come to believe that life is worth living only if we can give a meaning to it. Be comforted that even when his end was slowly approaching, he knew with conviction that freedom cannot flourish in the midst of ignorance.

Be comforted then that he died with the deepest conviction that civilization has not yet lost its battle against fanaticism. This was his last word and I am comforted in the sure knowledge that you would carry on after him and could not wrong your conscience. With my greatest sympathy.

Patricia

# About the Author

RAMIN JAHANBEGLOO is professor, vice dean, and executive director of Mahatma Gandhi Centre for Peace Studies, O.P. Jindal Global University, Sonipat, India. He is a philosopher who has worked extensively to foster constructive dialogue between divergent cultures. In his efforts to promote argumentative tradition, he has interacted with scholars and intellectuals from all over the world, such as the Dalai Lama, Noam Chomsky, Ashis Nandy, and George Steiner, among others. He has authored several books, which have been translated into different languages. Some of these include *Iran: Between Tradition and Modernity* (2004), *The Spirit of India* (2008), *The Gandhian Moment* (2013), *Time Will Say Nothing* (2014), and the series of conversations with prominent intellectuals, the latest being *Talking History: Romila Thapar in Conversation with Ramin Jahanbegloo with the Participation of Neeladri Bhattacharya* (2017).